In Veronica's Garden

In Veronica's Garden

by

Margaret Cadwaladr

MADRONA
Books & Publishing

Published by
Madrona Books & Publishing
P.O. Box 578, Qualicum, B.C., V9K 1T1
Fax: (250) 752-6934
Toll Free Orders: 1-800-866-5504
E-mail: inveronicasgarden@shaw.ca

Edited by Elizabeth McLean
Maps by Aaron Cadwaladr
Design by John McKercher
Typeset by The Typeworks
Set in Centaur & Legacy Sans

Printed and bound in Hong Kong by
C&C Offset Printing Co., Ltd.

NATIONAL LIBRARY OF CANADA CATALOGUING IN PUBLICATION DATA

Cadwaladr, Margaret, 1949–
 In Veronica's garden

 Includes bibliographical references and index.
 ISBN 0-9730096-0-8

 1. Milner Gardens and Woodland—History.   2. Gardens—British Columbia—
Qualicum Beach—History.   3. Milner, Veronica.   4. Qualicum Beach (B.C.)—
Biography.   I. Cadwaladr, Aaron.   II. Title.
SB466.C33M54 2002   971.1'204092   C2001-911708-6

For Jim

Primula Japonica ("Millers Crimson")

Contents

Introductory Note

M y mother was a larger than life personality and her character and spirit made a deep impression on her immediate family and friends. Her energy, determination and enterprise saved our ancestral home at Glin and when she went on to live in Canada after marrying my remarkable and benevolent stepfather Ray Milner she began to create the lovely garden beside the Strait of Georgia on Vancouver Island which is the focal point of this book.

These pages are a frank account of her life and background with very few blemishes brushed out. Some might think the book overcritical but I have always felt that a memorial must show the good and the bad as nothing is so uninteresting as a mere panegyric.

The story emphasizes her braveness and love of beauty and it gives me the greatest pleasure to think her garden in Qualicum Beach is in such caring hands tended by Malaspina University-

College. I am sure this legacy will give great pleasure to countless garden lovers.

I only hope that the house and gardens at Glin which my father and mother struggled so hard to keep going in very difficult times will also continue as a memorial to their efforts. It is exciting to think how much my wife Olda, and my eldest daughter Catherine, are doing every year to follow her example. Catherine, at the time of writing, has been studying garden history and working in the field of horticulture in Kew and Wisley. She seems to be following in her grandmother's footsteps!

Olda and I and our three daughters, Catherine, Nesta and Honor are pleased that Margaret has charted my beautiful mother's generous, determined, but often wayward path from her youth in England, her life at Glin and across the ocean and a continent to British Columbia in such a forthright and perspicacious manner.

Desmond FitzGerald
The Knight of Glin

Glin Castle.

Foreword

YOU MAY VERY WELL be asking yourself whether or not we really need another book about gardens. Please let me assure you that we do, especially this one, because you are about to experience a very interesting story involving some intriguing characters, their history, and their love for the development and cultivation of a woodlands garden.

This book is about vision, belief, opportunity, and persistence. International, national and provincial public interests as well as numerous community people played a role in preserving and enhancing a unique waterfront property on the eastern shores of Vancouver Island, British Columbia. You will find the story both fascinating and educational and it will give you some wonderful insights into the dreams of Ray, Rina and Veronica Milner and their friends during the last century, as they brought the project to fruition.

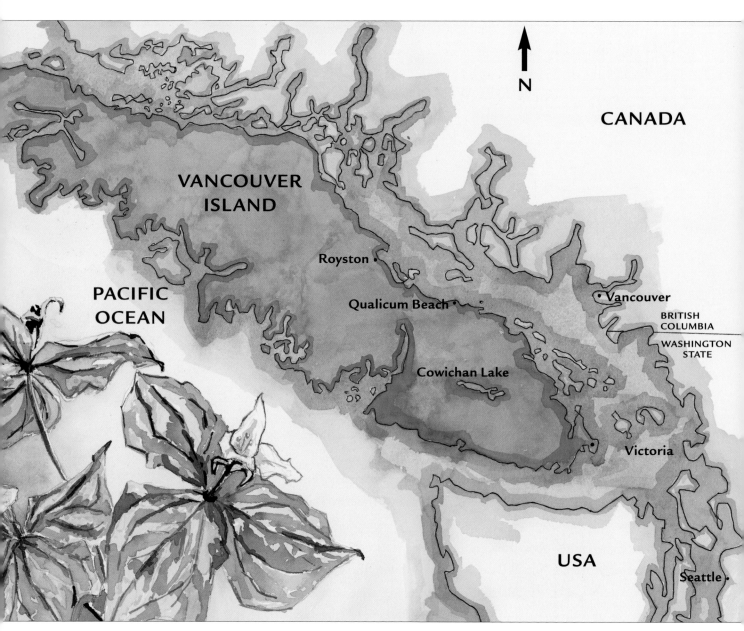

Map of Vancouver Island.

Foreword

This very special gardens and woodland, known by some as a wild garden, is situated in Qualicum Beach, where the salubrious climate, a term Veronica loved to use in describing the local weather conditions, provides ideal growing conditions for everything from very tall and ancient Douglas-firs to many hundreds of varieties of rhododendrons collected from all over the world.

When I read the first draft of the book, I couldn't put it down. I read it from cover to cover in one evening and wondered if my interest was stirred because I had played a part in this once-in-a-lifetime opportunity? Or, was it because the story was truly a riveting human-interest story, touching on everything from British royalty, to the development, history and acquisition of the garden? I believe it was a combination of both that kept my interest.

This book is not only well researched and well written, but also contains some excellent photographs that truly convey the total beauty of this oceanfront landscape and woodland garden. The author presents an accurate portrayal of the character of Veronica Milner, and an insightful description of how this woodland garden touched many of us as it evolved over time. Milner Gardens and Woodland has become an inspiration for those of us involved in its care, and its future.

Richard W. Johnston, President
Malaspina University-College
August 7, 2001

Aerial view of the Milner Gardens and Woodland.

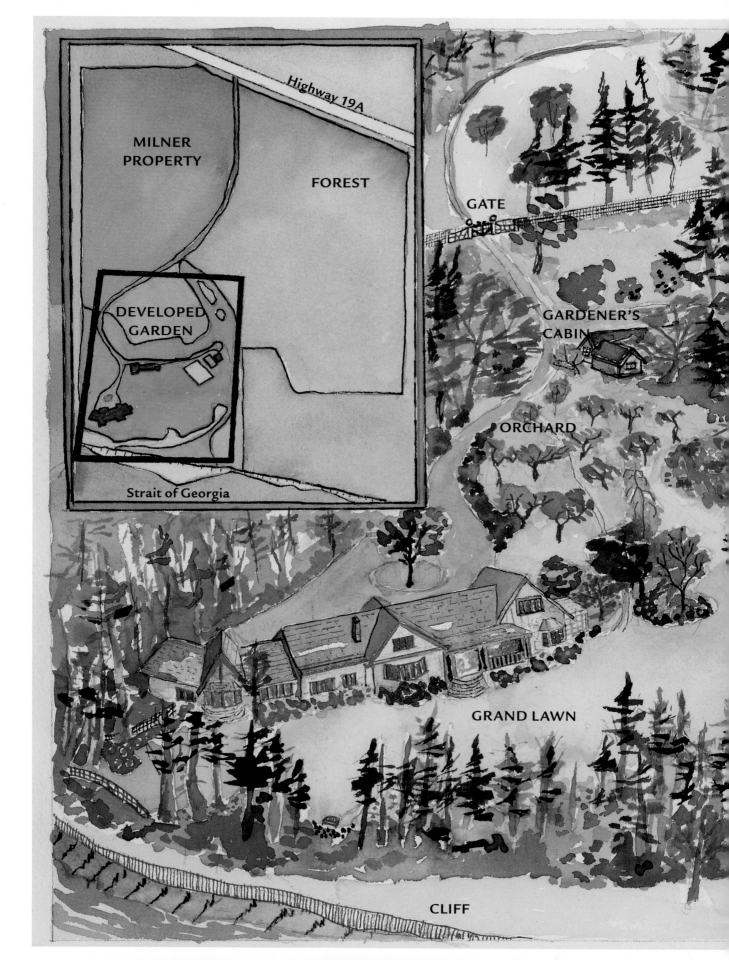

Highway 19A

MILNER
PROPERTY

FOREST

DEVELOPED
GARDEN

Strait of Georgia

GATE

GARDENER'S
CABIN

ORCHARD

GRAND LAWN

CLIFF

Preface

FIRST VISITED the garden on May 17, 1996. The day was rainy and cold. A piper and drummer began to play and, as if on cue, the clouds parted and the sun shone as Malaspina University-College began a ceremony to dedicate the Milner Gardens and Woodland. Veronica Milner, her knees tucked under a wool blanket, sat on the veranda surrounded by friends. About 200 guests sat below on folding chairs on the wet lawn. I sat in the second row with my husband Jim, then coordinator of the horticulture program at the University-College. The dignitaries made speeches. Jim presented Veronica with an honorary Certificate in Horticulture from Malaspina University-College. Finally, Veronica stood and gave a rambling speech about the garden and her late husband, Ray Milner.

When the crowd thinned, Jim and I went up to the veranda. Jim introduced me to this striking woman. Her eyes protruded as a result of thyroid problems. Her hair was blue rinsed. Despite her advanced years, she had a commanding presence. She reached up and took my hand. Hers was long and cool. Jim explained to Veronica that I was leaving for a trip to Ireland in a very few days. I could feel her rings as she pressed against my hand, pulling me toward her. "Come for tea before you go, my dear."

Later that week, we arrived for tea at four. She handed me a map drawn by her son when he was a boy. The thick black lines outlined the southwestern corner of Ireland. Glin Castle, where Veronica had lived for many years, was prominent. Afterwards, she took us on a tour of the house and garden, ending in the sunny "studio." Veronica, tired of leaning on her cane, sat in a chair as the afternoon flowed into a long May evening. She told us then, and often, that it was important that we understand her in order to understand the garden. When we left well after dark, we realized we had spent almost eight hours with her as she recounted her life story and the development of the garden in the most lucid manner she ever would.

Early in our relationship, Veronica invited herself to our house. The purpose of this outing was, in her words, "to see how you live." By happy chance, I served tea to Veronica in a teacup that had special meaning from her childhood. The pretty Ayns-

Veronica Milner with her dog Willow, September 1997.

ley cup was decorated with white and blue violets. Her nanny had allowed Veronica to serve tea to her dolls using identical cups if she was "very, very good." Veronica was a strong believer in predestination. The incident cemented our friendship and, I think, confirmed for Veronica that our relationship was indeed "meant to be."

Veronica had been looking for someone to write her biography for years. She made, apparently, several false starts. She had even attempted an autobiography. By coincidence, I had a long-standing interest in autobiography and life story and had taken an interdisciplinary graduate-level course at the

University of British Columbia on the topic. Veronica was certainly an available and intriguing subject. Although Malaspina did not have the funds to support this project, I went ahead and began research. It would be a shame, I felt, if her story did not live on. As I gained her trust, Veronica verbally authorized me to write the book and was very helpful in providing background materials. "Write that down," she would instruct. She gave me access to her personal photograph collection, scrapbooks, guest book and letters. Eventually, she gave me written permission to copy, display and publish photographs from her personal collection.

This book is a social history of the Milners' garden. As I began the research, it became clear that work in the garden preceded Veronica. Letters document her husband Ray's role in the early years. Ray and his first wife Rina owned the property for seventeen years before Veronica came along. Ray and Rina established a warm, inviting home and garden for their family and friends. Both loved the garden and forest. Noted rhododendron experts Ted and Mary Greig were involved with the garden before Veronica's time and several rhododendrons, magnolias, trees and plants were already established when Veronica arrived as a bride in 1954.

Jim and I developed a pattern that included weekly contact with Veronica. We were often invited for dinner or tea. Jim was obliged by his University-College position to spend time at the garden. As it happened, I was working part-time on short-term contracts at Malaspina University-College. I had the time and interest to devote to volunteering with this most unusual patron.

The sitting room was Veronica's command centre. She would hold court in a brocade chair raised on blocks of wood. Several pairs of glasses were suspended from coloured cords around her neck. She had a buzzer attached to the arm of the chair and would constantly ring for one of her helpers, giving orders. She had had hired help all her life, even when people were no longer willing to work "in service." In her later years, these employees were called "helpers" or "companions," although they certainly continued to play a de facto servant role. Veronica had no apparent empathy for them, dismissing and replacing them with stunning rapidity.

I met Veronica in her declining years and her memory was clearly failing. It was often impossible to ask her a question and get a direct answer. I found the best tactic was to mention a subject at tea, perhaps on Thursday, take note of her ramblings and research the subject as best I could before our next dinner together, usually on Saturday. The ability to converse at dinner was one of the social graces Veronica had learned well. She was most relaxed and comfortable at the dinner table. If I were able to put the material in context, she would respond appropriately to this "dinner conversation."

I devised a plan to gather information about the garden from Veronica. Tape recording or video was out of the question. Instead, I put a great many photographs of the garden in an album and would sit with her and take notes while she looked at them. The visual cues would trigger memories and keep her focused. The tactic worked so well that I began to bring picture books from the library of the Churchill family, the Edwardian era or any other topic I thought might jog her memory.

One story that illustrates the difficulties in interviewing Veronica was her story about her "favourite aunt." The problem was, she could not remember her aunt's name. She waved her hand in the air, the rings on her fingers flashing, "You know," she said, "those tea people." She went on to mumble something about flowers, which I couldn't quite catch. I dutifully noted in my little black book "flowers" and "those tea people." One day I found an obituary of one of Veronica's uncles. The American widow of another uncle, Lionel Guest, was the former Flora Bigelow! Aha! Aunt Flora must have been related to the New York tea merchants.

Within a week of meeting Veronica, I made my first trip to Ireland. While there, I visited Glin, the castle where Veronica had lived during her first marriage to Desmond FitzGerald, the Knight of Glin. I took a tour of the castle along with my mother and

The author and Desmond FitzGerald, the Knight of Glin in the garden at Glin Castle.

sister. As it happened, Veronica's son Desmond, the current Knight of Glin, was home. He escorted me through the garden on a warm spring afternoon, all the while telling me how difficult a person his mother was. I met Desmond again on several occasions and was in touch with him while his mother's health declined. After her death, Desmond provided me with additional letters and a box of slides taken in the garden over the years. He was very helpful to me in verifying family history and suggesting new avenues for research.

I mailed a copy of the first draft of the manuscript to Desmond. He and his wife Olda invited me to return to Ireland to continue my study, as he had several documents which would be valuable to the research. The FitzGeralds were extremely kind and generous to me during my second stay in Ireland. As well as suggesting some minor corrections to the manuscript, Desmond allowed me to view a huge number of personal letters and documents relating to his mother which he was in the process of handing over to the Special Collections department of the Gluksman Library at the University of Limerick. Desmond has both a personal and a professional interest in all aspects of Anglo-Irish history, art, country houses and gardens and was often able to quickly find just the right piece of research from his extensive library. We went over family photograph albums, discussed findings and rummaged through an old suitcase full of odds and ends from his mother's estate. He also arranged meetings with several people who knew his parents, or his mother, well. These included past and present employees, friends and relations. I visited the major sites of significance in Veronica's life in Ireland, including the Burren, Glin Castle, Foynes Flying Boat Museum, Killruddery House and Gardens, Adare Manor (now an exclusive luxury hotel), the National

Many, many letters written to Veronica between 1928–1998 are in the archives of the University of Limerick.

Botanic Gardens, Glasnevin, Dublin and the Mount Usher Gardens in County Wicklow.

Above all, Desmond allowed me access to his father's detailed diaries. Veronica gave her son his father's diaries shortly before her death. The five-year diaries span the years from 1925 until shortly before his death in 1949. The years 1933–1943 include, and sometimes consist of, small pocket diaries. These diaries chronicle the day-to-day life of the FitzGeralds' years in Ireland. They confirmed details that I had speculated about and opened the window to information about many artists, writers and prominent garden experts whose ideas influenced the development of the gardens in Qualicum Beach. These led to an understanding of the Milner Gardens and Woodland in the context of their class and times. The diaries also chronicle, in heartbreaking detail, Veronica Milner's dysfunctional first marriage.

I believe that the diaries are a highly factual source. Dates and facts, in many instances, can be cross-referenced with other published sources. Opinions and feelings are easily identified. I have included verbatim extracts from the diaries, with only minor spelling corrections. Interestingly, Veronica's husband, Desmond, wrote about his intentions in keeping the diaries after returning to Ireland in 1945 from a tuberculosis sanatorium in Arizona:

> . . . *[these diaries] will probably be of no interest to my family, but I have always tried to keep up these diaries which say little but may say a lot to*

Veronica's first husband, Desmond FitzGerald, the twenty-eighth Knight of Glin, kept detailed diaries.

the young ones, as to the way of life and the joys and unhappiness that all people must have during their lives. Should I depart soon [and my diaries] including this one and my previous ones are read, do not think that I am a bitter man, but I have had a very hard life, but I must admit with quite a lot of fun. So there it is.

Veronica told me that her home and garden was a place of peace and beauty, where there had never been any unhappiness. This seemed ludicrous, as the household was obviously often in the midst of great turmoil. Yet, for Veronica it was, indeed, an antidote for the ills of the modern world. She lived her life in a bubble. To visit her and the garden was to be transported to another time and place.

I was very fond of Veronica. I had the advantage of many years of professional experience in counselling-related jobs, as an inter-

viewer and in crisis intervention. These gave me the skills and experience to deal with the more unpleasant aspects of her personality. Veronica was a woman who seemed desperate to be understood. She often told me she felt out of place in Canada, even though it had been almost seventy years since she had lived in England. Canadians "don't speak the same language," she would often say. While some may feel the manuscript is too critical, or conversely, too generous, my mission has always been simply to understand. I have attempted to describe Veronica's long and interesting life in a fair and objective manner.

Acknowledgements

A TREMENDOUS AMOUNT of research is required for such a project. I spent a great deal of time interviewing Veronica's family and friends, both before and after her death. I spoke to friends, family members, enemies, employees and a member of the Royal Canadian Mounted Police. I had access to archival information, including a number of newsletters from Ray's business days that featured articles about him.

I am grateful to many individuals who helped me along the way with this project. Some were interviewed; some offered practical or emotional support. Others offered insights through casual conversation and reminiscences of Veronica. The long list includes, but is not limited to, Adare Manor Hotel and Golf Resort; Arul Amirtharaju; Geoff Ball; Leslie Bishop; Aaron, Dan and Jim Cadwaladr; the Canford School Archives; Lisa Collins and Florence Stephenson of Special Collections, Glucksman Library, University of Limerick; Allyne Cook; Nancy deCandole; Bob Duff and his staff at Glin Castle; Nancy Ellis; Olda and Desmond FitzGerald; Jean-Marc Fortier; Ross and Judy Fraser; Jim and Jean Greig; Annabelle Griffiths; Christopher Hands; David Harris; Tom Healy; Mary Hughes; Rich and Pat Johnston; Clive Justice; Eve Knight; Jonathan Lampman; Ursula Leslie; Dr. John LePage; May Liston; Sharon Lockhart; Sherwood and Maureen Marshall; Margaret Masse; The Dowager Countess of Meath; The Earl and Countess of Meath; Joan Magnusson; Charity Mewburn; Eliz-

abeth Mewburn; Robert Mewburn; Mary and Victor Miles; Phoebe Noble; Kristi Ozero; Sherry Prenger; Terry Preston; Patricia Roscoe; Dr. Reginald Roy; Marie Scoretz; Trudy Sorensen; Joe and Jane Stanhope; Drs. Roy and Janet Taylor; Dr. Lynn Van Luven; Charles Villiers; Judith Walker and Tom Wall.

The Malaspina University-College Research and Scholarship Committee funded my second trip to Ireland. I am indebted to the committee members, under the leadership of Dr. David Thomas, for this. I also wish to thank former Dean Sheila Colbert-Kerns for approving my application for funding. As well as offering advice, Margaret Horsfield and Peter Buckland inspired the manner in which the book was published. Rich and Pat Johnston and Jon

Acknowledgements

Lampman read the first completed draft. Jon also kindly read the revised version after my trip to Ireland. I am grateful to them all, and particularly to Rich Johnston for his enthusiasm and support for the project.

Above all, I am thankful to my son Aaron Cadwaladr and to Dr. Janet Taylor. Both read drafts with critical eyes and made suggestions that greatly improved the manuscript. Aaron painted the lovely maps while Janet was always ready to offer pieces of information she found while sorting the garden library as a volunteer. She also gathered relevant research from her own library and from other sources.

I do not pretend to be an expert in gardens or horticulture but several people who are experts offered their assistance. My husband Jim read many drafts of chapters and was my primary source in things horticultural. Dr. Roy L. Taylor read the final draft and assisted in establishing the correct names of plants. Clive Justice also corrected some errors. Landscape architect Judith Walker read my chapter on the development of the garden. In addition, Judy had started a project on the life of Mary Greig, so we were able to swap stories and information. This book is a social history, however, not a horticultural text, and any errors in plant identification are my own.

I could not have pulled this all together without the assistance of Vic Marks, John McKercher, indexer Charles Anderson and Elizabeth McLean, my editor. Thank you.

Finally, I am thankful that Veronica allowed me to share her extraordinary story.

CHAPTER ONE

The Garden

Had I a garden it should grow
Shelter where feeble feet
Might loiter long, or wander slow,
And deem decadence sweet;
Pausing, might ponder on the past,
Vague twilight in their eyes,
Wane calmer, comelier, to the last,
Then die, as Autumn dies.

— Alfred Austin

AS YOU SLOWLY WALK down the curving gravel drive, you anticipate the garden ahead. Around the next curve? No, still not there. Your eyes are drawn to the left and to the right by the forest: past thick trunks of western red-cedar (*Thuja plicata*) and Douglas-fir (*Pseudotsuga menziesii*); an understorey of salal (*Gaultheria shallon*), red huckleberry (*Vaccinium parviflorum*); and underneath, western sword fern (*Polystichum munitum*). Finally, stone pillars and iron gates say what they are meant to say: this is a place set apart, this is a world of its own, exclusive and private.

After the gate, another curved drive. To the left, an orchard is planted on an easy slope. A stand of Magnolia near the drive forms the transition from the orchard to the big house. Wisteria vines (*Wisteria sinensis*) with soft, plump flower clusters cling to its walls. The covered veranda looks out on both garden and sea views.

On the north side of the house, the garden borrows ideas and

1

practices from William Robinson's Victorian "Wild Garden," recreated and reinvented in the West Coast rain forest. Natural forms, grassy slopes, glimpses of ocean and water features appear amid native and exotic trees and shrubs. Form and structure dominate. Spring grass, intermingled with bulbs and wild flowers, is left to grow long. Trees are grouped to emphasize harmony and contrasts of size, colour and shape.

The garden slopes gently toward the sea, with a precipitous bluff plunging to the beach below. Breathtaking views of the Strait of Georgia are framed by old-growth Douglas-firs and red-cedars. Beyond the strait, the Coast Mountains of the British Columbia mainland can be seen. To the north, Denman, Hornby, Lasqueti and Texada islands are visible.

The multi-layered forest canopy casts a dense shade over much of the garden area. The understorey includes an extensive collec-

tion of rare rhododendrons as well as fine specimen trees. There are dark, secret places where the sun never shines. Formal areas feature lawn and border plants. A small orchard, and a berry and vegetable garden are tucked away. The garden includes specimens of Japanese and Full Moon maples (*Acer palmatum* and *Acer japonicum* 'Aconitifolium'), stewartia (*Stewartia pseudocamellia*), a dove tree (*Davidia involucrata*), cultivars of beech (*Fagus sylvatica*), birch (*Betula pendula*), golden chain tree

2

(*Laburnum x watereri* 'Vossii'), Katsura (*Cercidiphyllum japonicum*), dawn redwood (*Metasequoia glyptostroboides*) and Spanish chestnut (*Castanea sativa*).

Of the total forty-acre Milner Garden property (which was expanded to seventy acres in 1999), ten acres surrounding the house are developed garden; the rest is coastal Douglas-fir forest. A beach area lies at the bottom of the bluff. As well as the main house, the estate includes a swimming pool and pool house, tennis court, and gardener's cottage. There are areas of wildness where the garden merges with the forest in a kind of controlled neglect. Streams and meadow provide a further transition zone from the forest to the formal lawn. Blue herons fish the shore, while the dappled shade of the garden shelters songbirds. Purple finches and wrens nest in the camellias near the house. The garden features over 500 varieties of rhododendrons whose colours and textures contrast with the majestic forest trees.

The moods of the garden are limitless. Each season, each time of day holds a hidden treasure. The perennial smile of the cast bronze boy on the dolphin endures in rain, or sun, or under a cap of snow. He sails along on barren ground or surrounded by maidenhair fern, hostas, azaleas, daylilies and irises. Nearby, eighteenth-century bronze Chinese herons wade year-round in ponds, cooling their feet in the summer, raising their heads in the driving winter rains, and listening to the sounds of moving water.

Winter months are mild. Many of the trees have beautiful branch structures that the winter exposes, providing year-round interest. When the garden is blanketed with snow, the wet weight bends the rhododendrons. Snow and ice make the lines of the kiwi vine come alive. Luckily, West Coast snow is infrequent and doesn't last long. More often, rain softens or obscures the views and shines the leaves of rhododendrons. Winter clouds come and go. The air is full of the scent of damp soil. The dominance of the coniferous forest assures that the winter garden remains green. Mauve and burgundy hellebores (*Helleborus orientalis*) flowers appear. From the cold winter earth near the garden cottage, snowdrops, crocus and winter aconite (*Eranthus hyemalis*) promise the start of spring.

Spring arrives with bulbs and meadow flowers. Bluebells, lily-of-the-valley and forget-me-nots cluster under flowering fruit trees and magnolias (*Magnolia stellata, Magnolia x soulangeana*) in the meadow and orchard. In the forest, western trillium (*Trillium ovatum*) and anemone emerge. The meadow lawn is allowed to grow long with wild flowers: English daisy and buttercups, cyclamen, viola, and spring bulbs, scilla, glory-in-the-snow, winter aconite and daffodils. Each comes and goes in succession, or groups before the first cutting. Spring brings a sequence of hues: brilliant yellows, reds, oranges, blues and lavenders; washes of colour in painterly fashion. Camellias cluster near the house: pink, rose, and white. The colours, shapes, textures and size of hundreds of rhododendrons are astounding: delicate pink, purple *augustinii* hybrids, red May Day and *shilsonii*. Clouds of orange, purple, white, yellow, magenta — wave after wave of colour surges through the garden. Some rhododendrons have thin, delicate stems; others are thick and strong. Leaves are rounded or pointed, large or small. Giant Himalayan species are grouped together. In the thick, cool stands of rhododendrons, the drone of bees in blooms suspended in the air above your head can be heard. Petals spill on the ground to form an exotic carpet.

A quail and her covey of chicks might scurry from beneath the shelter of a low shrub, grunting and chuckling. Sweet smells drift on the air. The princess trees (*Paulownia tomentosa*) bloom high and out of reach, whereas *Clematis* (*montana* var. *rubens*) blooms along the tennis court gate.

By June, the garden is in transition. The great bursts of spring colour have passed. Only a few of the very large rhododendrons at the edge of the forest continue to flower. Blue-green hosta, fragrant honeysuckle, and delicate lacecap hydrangea cultivars (*Hydrangea macrophylla*) come into their own. If the light is just right, the golden leaves of the Katsura (*Cercidiphyllum japonicum*) shimmer in a shaft of warm sun.

The summer annuals in the cutting garden have not yet bloomed. Roses are just beginning. The hawthorn tree (*Crataegus* spp.) beside the gardener's cottage blooms with clusters of tight, red flowers. The Chinese dogwood (*Cornus kousa* var. *chinensis*) near the stream provides the most spectacular show. Tall trees protect the garden from the full heat of summer.

Days can be spent dreaming on the covered veranda, out of the hot sun, or wandering in the dappled shade of trails. Silence. From

time to time, sailboats propelled by the breeze drift by. If the tide is moving, waves lap on the shore. Three-foot-high geraniums in Chinese egg pots stand near the door to the house. Rudbeckia (*Rudbekia fulgida* 'Goldstrum') blooms along the pool fence. Roses add fragrant colour to the summer garden as well as cut flowers for the house. Their charming blooms will last into the fall. A hummingbird might dart so close to you that you feel the wind of its wings in your hair.

During autumn, the garden is ablaze with foliage. The fiery red Japanese maple is a focal point, rich scarlet against brilliant yellows. *Fothergilla major* and purple-leaf flowering plum (*Prunus cerasifera* 'Pissardi') add complexity to the palette. Plump, sweet golden plums and apples ripen in the orchard. If the glory bower tree (*Clerodendrum trichotomum*) is in bloom, you might stop to crush its leaves in your hands, releasing the smell of peanut butter. Roses begin to fade, but retain a soft beauty. The exfoliating bark of the paperbark maple (*Acer griseum*) provides interest as it peels and feathers, exposing new flesh underneath.

The significance and complexity of the estate go beyond the

garden's aesthetic richness, however. The property is located within the coastal Douglas-fir biogeoclimatic zone, which is limited to a small portion of southeastern Vancouver Island, some of the Gulf Islands, and a narrow strip along the mainland coast. These forests were once dominated by towering Douglas-fir, western red-cedar, and grand fir. Deforestation has been extensive due to logging and agriculture and is increasing due to the rapid expansion of residential development. Less than one percent of the original old-growth forest remains and much of the existing second-growth forest has lost its biodiversity. The sixty acres of forest beyond the garden, and intermingling with it, is relatively undisturbed. As a result, this estate has a very high conservation value. It is an awe-inspiring remnant of a fast-vanishing ecosystem. Strolling through this quiet place, you wonder at the age and size of the giant trees and are thankful they have been spared.

As evening falls, a dramatic shift in mood occurs. Long shadows fall across the grand lawn, intensifying the sound of waves on the beach below. The lights of fish boats returning to the marina at French Creek glide across the water. As you leave the garden, you pause to wonder who created this haven of beauty and strength, of order and chaos, out of the forest? Who possessed the skill and art to create the relaxed elegance of this hidden place? Who had the vision to preserve it?

CHAPTER TWO

Veronica

Not wholly in the busy world, nor quite
Beyond it, blooms the garden that I love.
News from the humming city comes to it
It sounds of funeral or of marriage bells.

— Alfred, Lord Tennyson

ERONICA VILLIERS was born in London, England on February 16, 1909 at about half past eight in the evening. Descended from a long line of aristocratic men and women, she grew up with a clear idea of her place in the social hierarchy. Although she never held a title herself, she was extremely proud to be part of the British aristocracy and of the people she encountered in her long life. "I am not important," Veronica told me. "My importance is only because I was associated with important people."

The root of the word "aristocracy" is from the Greek *aristos* and literally means rule by the best citizens, a concept she held dear throughout her life. The aristocracy consider themselves both different from and better than others. Veronica decried the democratic concept of rule by the people as rule "by the bottom." She had an imperious manner and insisted on judging whether those she met "knew how to behave." Although Veronica claimed, "it's not who you are, but what you are," she was, in fact, acutely aware of, and concerned with, class, race and pedigree. She was nostalgic for the past of leisured money. To her, the British Empire was a symbol of England's material and spiritual greatness, the proof of its evolutionary superiority. In Veronica's opinion, the "top of the top" ruled the Empire, and much of the world, with wisdom and harmony.

Curiously, Veronica was related on both maternal and paternal sides to the Villiers, the once powerful Norman family whose story is woven through the history of England. As both Winston Churchill, her mother's cousin, and Veronica are descended from the first Duke of Marlborough, they are related to the late Diana, Princess of Wales. Marlborough's daughter, Lady Anne Churchill, married Charles Spencer, third Earl of Sunderland. Her children included Charles, who became the third Duke of Marlborough, and John Spencer, whose son became the first Earl Spencer. Veronica and Winston Churchill were descended from the Duke of Marlborough, while Diana was descended from the Spencer line.

Veronica came from a line of formidable women. On her maternal side, one of her early family members was Barbara Villiers, Duchess of Cleveland (1641–1709), and a mistress of King Charles II. Barbara bore five of the king's illegitimate children in five years and is described as "a woman of great beauty, but most enormously vicious and ravenous." Veronica seemed, however, to identify most strongly with two more recent women, her maternal great-grandmother, Lady Charlotte Guest, and her maternal grandmother, Lady Wimborne, the former Cornelia Spencer-Churchill.

Veronica's great-grandmother, Lady Charlotte Guest (1812–

1895), was a self-taught writer who was known for her translation of the *Mabinogin*, a three-volume collection of medieval Welsh poems and legends. She taught herself Greek, Latin and Welsh and worked on the translations during her numerous pregnancies. Both Lord Tennyson and Matthew Arnold claimed to owe a debt of gratitude to Lady Charlotte for her work.

Charlotte met Benjamin Disraeli, the writer and future Prime Minister of England, at an opera. He considered marriage with Charlotte, though apparently not for the most noble of reasons. He wrote to his sister: "By the bye, how would you like Lady Z [Charlotte Bertie, Veronica's great-grandmother] for a sister-in-law, very clever, 25,000 pounds and domestic? As for 'love' all my friends who married for love and beauty either beat their wives or live apart from them. This is literally the case. I may commit many follies in life, but I never intend to marry for 'love,' which I am sure is a guarantee of infelicity." His sister was horrified, not at the thought of marital violence, but at his choice of partners: "What improvident blood more than half fills her veins." His sister need not have worried. At twenty-one, Lady Charlotte Bertie married forty-eight-year-old, very wealthy John Guest on July 29, 1833 at St. George's Church, Hanover Square, London. Guest was a man "in trade," and therefore looked down upon by society. Ironically, Disraeli married for love, an apparently happy situation, while Charlotte married an older man of lower social status for wealth.

John Guest owned Dowlais Ironworks in the south Wales coalfields near Merthyr Tydfil. With eighteen blast furnaces, it was the largest ironworks in the world at the time. When John died in 1852, Charlotte was left a widow with ten children. She took over the management of the family business, a tremendous and extraor-

Rhododendron augustinii.

dinary feat for a Victorian woman. "I am iron now — and my life is altered into one of action, not of sentiment," she wrote at the time.

Lady Charlotte's life was full of contradictions. On the one hand, the steel mills at Dowlais were progressive. She established a workmen's library, sponsored a recreation area for workers and evening cultural events featuring poetry, politics, piano and paternalism. A program of sickness, old age and death benefits, based on equal employer-employee contributions to a fund, was set up. She established showpiece schools in Dowlais in the 1850s, the total capital cost of which equalled that of the government budget for school construction in all of England and Wales in 1833. These innovative schools educated girls and young women, as well as boys and men. Yet despite these progressive developments, Dowlais had deplorable housing and sanitation. In 1849, over 500 people died of cholera in the town. In 1854, another epidemic swept the area and Dowlais had the highest mortality rates in the kingdom. John Martin, who illustrated Milton's *Paradise Lost,* had visited Dowlais. Charlotte's biographers Revel Guest and Angela John quote the *Morning Chronicle* which suggested he might have been inspired by the smoky, steaming, fire and roar of machines for his portrait of Dante's Dis, or hell.

Lady Charlotte is perhaps best known for her collections of porcelain, fans, and *objects d'art.* Much of her collection is displayed in the Victoria and Albert Museum in London where it is known as the Schreiber Collection. The collection is named after her second husband Charles Schreiber, her children's tutor, whom she married in 1855.

Veronica's maternal grandmother was Winston Churchill's very wealthy aunt, Lady Wimborne, Cornelia Spencer-Churchill, eldest

daughter of the seventh Duke of Marlborough. Cornelia was attractive, intelligent and artistic. The regal Cornelia married Lady Charlotte's eldest son, Ivor Guest. She was intensely interested in politics and often sat in the iron grill-covered ladies' gallery in the House of Commons. She gave political advice to her nephew, Winston Churchill, which he valued and followed.

The Churchills had a great deal of involvement with Veronica's family. Winston Churchill had both affection for, and loyalty to, his extended family. Although Veronica only met him once, she knew his wife Clementine quite well, she said. The Guests helped the Churchills out financially and provided accommodations on more than one occasion. Biographer William Manchester notes that when, as so often was the case, money was short in the Churchill household, the Guest family came to the rescue. At one point, Winston and Clementine moved into Veronica's grandmother's house at 3 Tenterden Street, near Hanover Square. Later, they moved in with Cornelia's son Freddie and his wealthy American wife, the former Amy Phipps, at 2 Sussex Square, a block from Victoria Gate, Hyde Park.

Clementine was, however, not impressed with Winston's relations. When the Churchills needed money, she sold the beautiful diamond necklace Cornelia had given her as a wedding present. When Lady Cornelia invited the couple to her estate at Canford, Winston pleaded with Clementine in a letter quoted by Manchester: "I have a great regard for her – & we have not too many friends. If however you don't want to go – I will go alone. Don't come with all your hackles up & your fur brushed the wrong way – you naughty." Clementine replied, "I will write tomorrow to Aunt Cornelia – & I will be very good I promise you, especially if you

Canford was the country home of Veronica's grandmother and great grandmother.

stroke my silky tail." Once, while playing bridge with Winston and Clementine at Canford, Ivor threw the deck of cards at Clementine, hitting her on the forehead. Clementine quickly responded by leaving the table, going to bed, and packing up for London early the next morning.

Clementine especially disliked Ivor and Freddie Guest. It seems that others shared Clementine's opinion of Veronica's Uncle Freddie. Historian David Cannadine noted that: "Even his *Times* obituary hinted that Freddie Guest was not a nice man to know."

As a young and impressionable girl, Veronica visited the splendid country estate of Canford, where both Lady Charlotte and Lady Cornelia had lived. As an old woman, Veronica kept a faded, unframed photograph of Canford on her mantlepiece in Qualicum. She often spoke of both her grandmother and great-grandmother, and would proudly show various items she had inherited from them. Veronica married Ray Milner in the same London church where both Lady Charlotte and Lady Cornelia were married and had swans, the emblem on the Wimborne crest, throughout the Milner house. The sitting room featured swans on the light fixtures. She had glass and porcelain swans in her bedroom, the sitting room, and the dining room.

Veronica, a lonely and neglected child, was attracted to the strong personalities of these powerful, intelligent women and seemed to have inherited their formidable willpower. As well as strength of character, they had wealth, which, as Veronica would say, is of "…no use in itself, but important because of what you can do with it." Interestingly, both women used their money, in part, to leave a legacy in education. While Charlotte had established schools in Dowlais, Cornelia founded the Church Education Corporation, dedicated to the establishment of boarding schools for girls. In 1923, she sold her estate at Canford for use as a boys' public school.

Veronica's family history was both a blessing and a curse. Her family gave her a love of art and beauty, and connections to wealth and those with powerful positions in society. They gave her a love of gardens. Although the family had wealth and often power, it also had problems, including a long history of erratic behaviour and mental illness. Churchill was well known for the "black dogs" of depression that hounded him. Many considered him unstable and arrogant. Biographer R.F. Foster notes that Churchill had "manic swings of mood" throughout his life. Guest and John relate that Lady Charlotte herself was prone to periods of depression and her brother's sanity was questionable. The family struggled with the question of whether to have him, the only male, declared incompetent. The dysfunctional nature of Veronica's family has been well documented. Cannadine reported they had an "above average amount of infidelity, divorce, erratic behaviours, sexual scandal…" Ivor Guest, Veronica's grandfather was an "incorrigible snob and social climber," who had a temper and was impulsive. He was known as "the paying guest." Foster describes how Benjamin Disraeli made Ivor First Baron Wimborne in 1880. "Disraeli, approached by the Marlboroughs on his behalf, could only ask 'what has he done?'" In a footnote, Foster noted that Disraeli added, "nothing would give me greater pleasure than to place a coronet on the brow of dear Cornelia."

According to Cannadine, there was a prevailing view that the Churchill family was "unstable, unsound and untrustworthy." Gladstone shared this sentiment. In 1882, he declared, "There never was a Churchill from John of Marlborough down that had either morals or principles." Ivor was a pompous man and often parodied. His son, also named Ivor Guest, was also mocked:

> *One must suppose that God knew best*
> *When he created Ivor Guest.*

A rather sacrilegious prayer of the same era goes:

> *Grant, O Lord, eternal rest*
> *To thy servant Ivor Guest.*
> *Never mind the where or how,*
> *Only, Lord, let it be now.*

Cornelia Spencer-Churchill was a wily and manipulative woman, suggested her great-grandson Desmond FitzGerald. Cornelia carefully assessed marriage partners for her many children. The daughters married peers; the sons married wealthy Americans.

This practice was not unusual in Victorian and Edwardian times. In fact, it was so common that a directory was developed for wealthy Americans seeking eligible, titled spouses for their offspring. Elaine, Veronica's mother, refused to accept the practice of arranged marriages and held out for years to marry Ernest Villiers (1863–1923), presumably for love.

Ernest, a second son of a second son, was not a wealthy man. His claim to the Villiers name was actually tenuous and resulted from either an illegitimate liaison or a secret marriage. Her grandfather and his only sister were what were known as "children of the mist." Ernest's father, the Rev. Charles Villiers, rector of Croft in Yorkshire, was the son of Thomas Hyde Villiers, MP, a very brilliant and promising politician who died young in 1832. Charles's elder brother became the fourth Earl of Clarendon in 1838, and was Viceroy of Ireland between 1847 and 1852, during the worst years of the famine. Charles and his sister were brought up under the name of Lawrence by their grandmother, Mrs. George Villiers. *Burke's Peerage* notes that Queen Victoria allowed them to adopt the Villiers name in February 1839.

Ernest Villiers became a clergyman and then went into politics, and served as Member of Parliament for Brighton from 1906 to 1910. During Veronica's very early childhood, the family divided their time between London and their home at 41 Adelaide Crescent, Hove, a small town adjacent to Brighton. Villiers was an articulate orator but neither enjoyed nor excelled at the fast-paced London life, nor at politics. When Veronica was still a small child, her father was forced to retire from politics by his mother-in-law Cornelia in favour of one of her sons, the infamous Freddie Guest. The family was apparently given an adequate, but not generous,

allowance. Many years later, when Veronica was complaining to her mother that her sister was shown favouritism, Elaine wrote: "No one has suffered from injustice (parental) in her youth more than myself as I had very much less than my sisters in every way & your father's career was killed for the sake of my brothers. I did not curse but we resolved therefore to be as impartial as possible between you all…"

Despite whatever difficulties they faced, Veronica's parents loved gardens, a love they shared with their friend Poet Laureate Alfred Austin (1835–1913). Although many mocked his poetry, Austin's prose work *The Garden That I Love* (1894) was a popular success. Veronica was named from a companion volume *In Veronica's Garden*, published in 1896. Early editions of both were among Veronica's most prized possessions. Veronica's parents built a country house, Hambrook Park, near the West Sussex town of Chichester. Photos of the garden show geometrical beds in a formal style. By the time Veronica married in 1929, the family had moved to Combe Bissett, near Salisbury.

Like other aristocratic children in the Edwardian age, Veronica saw little of her parents. They were distant entities and servants were central to her life. As was the custom in upper-class families of the time, uniformed nannies and nursemaids raised her and her siblings, two bothers and a sister, in the top floor of the house. A nanny was responsible for dressing and undressing the children, playing with them and taking them for walks. Every day at teatime, Veronica, known by the unlikely nickname "Nixy," was scrubbed and dressed in her best frock and allowed to join her mother for a short time in the drawing room. Veronica was a difficult child for servants to control. Her nephew recalled her laughing recollec-

Hambrook Hall,
showing the gardens.

tions of the brief and turbulent stays of some nineteen gov-
ernesses. Veronica's parents were also frequently away. When she
was young, they went on an extended trip around the world. The
family speculates that some very unhappy or traumatic event in
Veronica's childhood might have been the cause of many enduring
problems in her life. She clearly had a sometimes-volatile nature
and an excessive self-centredness. Whether from a single event, un-
due discipline or neglect, her behaviour appeared to mask underlying feelings of inadequacy that she was never able to overcome.

Veronica was extremely jealous of her sister Barbara, ten years
her senior, whom she felt was the favourite child. Barbara married
Brigadier General Sir Smith Hill Child, second and last Baronet
of Newfield, Knight of the Grand Cross of the Royal Victorian
Order and Companion of the Order of Bath in December 1925.
Child was Master of the Household to King George VI, a most
important post in royal circles. After an incident in London in the
early 1950s, in which Veronica apparently went on a jealous rage,
her mother wrote to her: "I had so looked forward to seeing you

again & it was a bitter disappointment to find that you had nothing but jealousy and bitterness…" She resolved never to have Veronica and Barbara together in the same house again.

Whatever unhappiness existed, it was clear that Veronica loved the country life. Childhood days always included a trip to the park. Nanny would push the pram, and she and Veronica would collect hawthorn thorns that would be fashioned into pens for drawing. Her happiest times were spent playing in the garden, and she especially remembered violets. If she was "very, very good," nanny allowed Veronica to serve tea to her dolls using the fine china teacups with a pattern of white and blue violets that I was later to reintroduce.

Veronica often visited her grandmother's estate at Canford and spent many happy hours as a young girl in the gardens there. It must have made an overpowering impression on a young girl to walk into the 11,000-acre Dorset estate near Wimborne that had been purchased by Lady Charlotte in 1846. Parts of the manor house were first built in 1220. In 1848 an addition was built, an adaptation by Sir Charles Barry, architect of the British Houses of Parliament. Veronica and her family lived in an elegant, but relatively modest, home. The great hall of Canford, on the other hand, measures seventy feet long by thirty-six feet across, with sixty-foot-high ceilings complemented by rich carvings, crystal chandeliers and stained-glass windows.

An elaborately carved, walnut staircase led from the north side of the hall. The long gallery was used to display various art treasures, their famous silver and porcelain collections, fine furniture, and the family coat of arms. A porcelain swan sat near the fireplace. Outside, a 100-foot tower, decorated with the family coat of arms, rose over the main entrance. A bell tower, housing a Dutch bell cast in 1592, completed the scene. These features gave Canford the air of dignified authority popular in Victorian, aristocratic properties. In 1851, the house employed a tutor, governess, house steward, coachmen, grooms, footmen, labourers, nurses, cooks, a "still-room" maid, three laundry maids, assorted housemaids and a kitchen maid.

The gardens were equally impressive. The driveway to the estate was, according to Veronica, "seven miles long" and lined with rhododendrons "as tall as trees." Veronica clearly remembered riding on spring afternoons with her grandmother through flowering rhododendrons. Built on the south bank of the River Stour, Canford boasted several leafy lanes and a large glass-roofed tennis court, built by Veronica's grandfather, Ivor. When Veronica was a child, a beautiful tree-lined walk extended from the kitchen gardens to a nearby vicarage. The park garden featured fine trees including tulip trees, cork oak, sweet gum and two trees of special note, the Mountjoy oak and the Great chestnut. The Mountjoy oak was already considered ancient in notes written by Captain Francis Grose in 1785. The Great chestnut remains the sole survivor of a group of four Spanish chestnuts in the estate. The tree, when measured in December 1925, was thirty-nine and a half feet in circumference.

From the age of approximately twelve, Veronica attended her grandmother's Sandecotes School. This was one of three girls' schools established by Lady Cornelia as part of the Church Education Corporation. Each catered

Veronica attended Sandecotes School. This photograph was taken approximately a year after she left the school.

Winter aconite.

to a particular class of students. One was for the elite, another was for upper middle-class girls (the daughters of lawyers, physicians and the like), and the third was open to more "common" girls. Sandecotes catered to the middle group. The three schoolhouses, nestled amid treed gardens, were at Parkston, near Bournemouth and about ten miles from Canford. According to Nancy de Candole, a pupil at the school shortly after Veronica's time, the strict headmistress, Miss Granger-Grey, was an eccentric. Well into the 1920s, she continued to wear the long dresses of the Edwardian era. Photographs show stern-faced teachers and uniformed girls.

It was a strict, enclosed life. The girls rarely left the grounds and were lucky if they saw their parents once during the year. On Saturdays in summer, the girls walked three miles to the oceanside, always under the close supervision of school staff. The school placed a very large emphasis on scripture and the girls attended prayers every morning and evening and church three times on Sunday. They had three uniforms: white and navy for everyday, bright scarlet skirts and red ties for formal occasions, and red for gym. White was allowed on the tennis court. They wore black tights they learned to darn themselves. The girls wore black shoes every day; brown was tolerated on Sundays. Choir, lawn tennis and drama kept them occupied in off hours and when they were not busy with church or studies. Miss Granger-Grey was a lover of the English language and Shakespeare. They studied English literature, French and German. The only science lessons they had were in botany and Veronica's schoolmates, now more horticulturally sophisticated, called her "Veronica Japonica."

Even as a young girl, Veronica was strong-willed. She did not tolerate the strict discipline of school life well. After approximately a year and a half at the boarding school, a teacher made the mistake of suggesting that Veronica's hands were not clean. Veronica was insulted. I can imagine her asking, "Don't you know who I *am*?" in an incredulous voice. She planned with a friend to run away. When the friend did not appear at the designated hour, Veronica left alone, walking miles in the bush beside the road, so as not to be seen. On the way, she stopped at a railway station. The stationmaster questioned where she was travelling all alone. Incredibly, he seemed to believe her explanation that she was travelling to Brighton. She continued walking several miles to Canford, her grandmother's estate. Grandmother responded to the small figure on her doorstep with an abrupt call for her driver, hat and gloves. It was an immediate return to school for the runaway. Veronica's formal education soon ended, however. She finished the term and did not return to Sandecotes.

Veronica, whether she knew it or not, was following in her cousin Winston's footsteps. One of his biographers, Robert Lewis Taylor, wrote: "Neither in fact nor in fiction is there to be found precisely that quality of volcanic rebellion which characterised nearly all his action… Whatever Churchill did (and he accomplished wonders) he did on purpose." When he first attended an expensive and fashionable school at Ascot, it was "an institution that was critically shaken by the experience." One can see that Churchill blood flowed in Veronica's veins. "It's not for nothing that I'm a Churchill," as she would say.

Veronica's sister, Barbara, ten years older, also attended Sandecotes School. Like Veronica, Barbara kept aloof from the other girls. Although merely "poor relations" of Lady Wimborne, both were "grand dames" of the school, recalled Nancy de Candole.

Neither participated in sports. Barbara, however, did not take such extreme measures as Veronica. She stayed at the school for about four years, completing her education.

Veronica "finished" her education in Europe, studying music and German in Dresden, art and French in France, and music in Lucerne. In evenings around the table, the young women spoke French and German, reciting poetry. Late in life, she would still slip into French, a habit fashionable in the early part of the twentieth century. She also enjoyed her music studies. In pre-television days, the piano was a central focus of entertainment. Veronica was, she told me, "thought to have a lovely voice."

Veronica also studied "domestic science." This subject was designed to teach young upper-class women how to manage the large household that would result from the inevitable marriage. Although never expected to perform household tasks, her education included such domestic duties as making tea. As Veronica pointed out, "one cannot supervise others if one doesn't understand the chore." Veronica prided herself on never having cooked or cleaned. Servants remained central to her life, even when few could afford such luxuries. At age eighty-eight, she proudly proclaimed that although all of her friends have had their "hands in the dishwater," she never had.

In Europe, Veronica's sometimes difficult nature rose again. The housemistress in Lucerne thought she was "impossible." Veronica claimed that she was beaten with sticks on her arms. "It was horrible," she told me. She complained about the treatment to her mother, but Elaine would not believe it, or perhaps thought that Veronica was deserving of it. Corporal punishment was not unusual at the time, even in the upper classes. In any event, the ever resourceful Veronica came up with a plan. She would spend "an hour and a half in the loo," claiming to be stricken with constipation. She climbed out the bathroom window, and down the drainpipe, to freedom.

Her family connections brought exciting opportunities for the young girl. In January 1923, when she was thirteen, she travelled to Scotland to visit her mother's friend, a lady-in-waiting to the queen. There, the twenty-two-year old Elizabeth Bowes-Lyon announced her engagement to Prince Albert George, the Duke of York. Young Veronica saw the beautiful bride-to-be and her betrothed, the future king and queen, in a tiny chapel on a royal estate.

Veronica "came out" in an age when the term meant formal admittance to, and acceptance in, society. Aristocratic families had an inherited right to be presented at court. A strict code of behaviour was enforced, and most young women entered marriage completely ignorant about sex and childbirth. Young girls who had lived like nuns were suddenly plunged into a courting ritual. Veronica herself had had little contact with boys outside the family. "The Season" was an opportunity to meet suitable young men, and was extremely important, especially to young women of social status but no personal wealth. Marriage was the only route to financial security. The goal was to marry well, and a girl was deemed successful if she became engaged in her first season. Veronica took this goal seriously, apparently, and many years later still blushed to remember proposing to a Lord. (In gentlemanly fashion, he turned her down, protesting they were both too young for marriage.)

Veronica was presented at Buckingham Palace wearing a white satin dress and the de rigeur white Prince of Wales feathers. Never allowed out without the company of her mother or brother as

chaperon, she stayed in London for "The Season," the spring and early summer months of May, June and July. She attended balls, luncheons, dinners and dances with carefully selected young guests. Formal evening gown designs were carefully kept secrets, so as to attract attention when the girl entered the ballroom. The men wore white ties and tails.

Veronica came out with her cousin of the same age, Diana, daughter of her wealthy Aunt Amy and Uncle Freddie Guest. Her American aunt was the daughter of Henry Phipps, business partner of Andrew Carnegie and considered one of the ten wealthiest women in America. Veronica, however, always had a loathing of the nouveau riche and their conspicuous displays of wealth. She abhorred "vulgarity." Old money preferred understated, low-key elegance. Aunt Amy took Diana on a buying trip to Paris for gowns. "Poor Diana," said Veronica, "had to wear those awful Paris gowns and pearls as big as eggs." She was less unhappy that Aunt Amy paid for many of the parties and balls the young women attended. "We were spoiled," she recalled. At Ascot, Diana wore a large pink hat made of crinoline material. This proved to be a poor choice in the wet English weather. It rained, and the hat melted in a hideous mess around her head.

Veronica's coming out was in the age of the so-called "Bright Young Things" of the 1920s when the younger members of the upper classes rebelled against their strict Victorian parents. Many of the eligible young men had died during the war and the aristocracy had begun to decline. While others pushed the limits of good behaviour and good taste, Veronica's parents kept her on a rather short leash. Although she attended dances at fashionable hotels that lasted until dawn, the affairs were likely stiff, heavily chaperoned events. Men of good manners still stood when a woman entered the room. Most girls were not allowed to wear powder on their nose and were never allowed in mixed company unless chaperoned.

Veronica met her future husband in the library at Killruddery House, Bray, County Wicklow in Ireland on Wednesday, August 8, 1928. Killruddery was the country estate of his relatives the Earl and Countess of Meath. A group was attending a car rally, one of many such events she attended with Charles Amherst Villiers, her eccentric brother. Amherst was trained as a physicist at Cambridge and became a brilliant inventor. In 1925, he supercharged some of the more advanced cars of the day. His work on the Bentley made the car a legend at Brookslands and LeMans in 1929. It could reach speeds of over 138 miles per hour.

Desmond FitzGerald was a dashing young Anglo-Irishman who had spent much of the twenties in London and Paris. It was the era of the "lost generation" of disillusioned young Americans and Britons in the post–Great War period. Cars were the rage in the 1920s and Desmond shared this obsession with Amherst. As well as racing fast cars, Desmond's passions were sailing, fishing and hunting. Handsome and extremely fastidious about his appearance, he is seen in photographs as a young man wearing tweed upon tweed, an inevitable cigarette between his fingers. Desmond was, however, a sickly young man. On June 6, 1928, he noted in his diary that he went to see his doctor. "He now is again not quite sure what the trouble is."

By Saturday, August 11, 1928, Desmond was in love. "Have lost head altogether over Veronica," he wrote in his diary. His life, he wrote, had been "permanently jolted." The next Thursday he was

Veronica and Desmond
wed on January 9, 1929.

busy acting as chauffeur to Lord Meath and Sir Robert Baden-Powell, the British soldier and founder of the Boy Scout and Girl Guide movements in the nearby gardens at Powerscourt. His diary entry is as follows: "A very busy afternoon driving Lord Meath & Baden Powell through the scout camps at Powerscourt. Veronica is on my mind all the time, will write to her as soon as I get home." Soon after, he proposed to Veronica in the back seat of Amherst's car. "Well, I suppose we may as well marry," Veronica recalled he said to her. He wrote in his diary: "The most wonderful thing in the world happened. She loves me & I love her." He worried, however, that she would be unhappy in his isolated and "old, shabby and dilapidated house," the relatively inferior Glin Castle.

On January 9, 1929, a month before her twentieth birthday, Veronica married Desmond Windham Otho FitzGerald, the future twenty-eighth Knight of Glin, of Glin Castle, County Limerick, Ireland. Desmond and Veronica were married in St. Peter's Church, Eaton Square, London. Splendid in her floor-length white gown and lace veil, Veronica wore a long string of pearls and carried a large bouquet of lilies, held together by a satin sash. She was given away by her brother Amherst and five bridesmaids attended her. Five hundred guests celebrated the wedding at a reception at Wimborne House, the town "palace" in London, now belonging to her aunt and uncle. The reception took place entirely by candlelight, "not a single electric light," as Veronica recalled. The happy couple honeymooned in Paris, Rome and Naples and ended their trip on the Island of Capri.

Early Years in Ireland

No one worth possessing
Can be quite possessed;
Lay that on your heart,
My young angry dear;
This truth, this hard
and precious stone,
Lay it on your hot cheek,
Let it hide your tear.

—Sara Teasdale

GLIN CASTLE was built on the southern shores of the Shannon estuary, about thirty miles west of Limerick. The Fitz-Gerald family originally came to Ireland from Wales as mercenaries in the 1170s and built their first castle near Glin around 1200. The current building was erected in the 1780s near the ruined keep where generations of ancestors had lived. Money, however, was a problem from the start. The knight inherited a great deal of debt along with the estate. The third floor was never finished, and much of the original contents of the castle had been sold in a bankruptcy sale in 1803. In the 1820s and 30s, however, three sets of Gothic lodges, battlements and a hermitage were built. The Georgian house was transformed into a castle.

Money continued to be a problem for the knights of Glin. The famine years of the 1840s, of course, devastated the country. Anglo-Irish power had been declining throughout the Victorian

Aerial view of
Glin circa 1950.

era. Reform legislation, the disestablishment of the Church of Ireland, the widening of the voting franchise, tenants' rights, and radical land legislation all had an impact. Young Anglo-Irish men had traditionally served as officers in the British army and colonial services. During the Great War, many of these young Anglo-Irish, along with many Irish, died in the trenches of France. The Dowager Lady Meath reflected that this resulted in an abundance of "lonely sisters left in crumbling houses, roaming from one damp room to another."

Veronica moved to Ireland only five years after the end of the Irish Civil War. In Dublin, horse-drawn cabs were common. Green letterboxes had replaced British red and the countryside was littered with burned and abandoned country houses, their gardens left to weeds. The FitzGeralds were the only Protestants in a Catholic town. With the departure of the Anglo-Irish, the Protestant population in Ireland had declined from over ten per cent to barely three per cent. Each Sunday, they attended St. Paul's, the small Victorian church in a grove of beeches just outside the castle gates. The tiny church, built in 1865, has beautiful Pre-Raphaelite stained-glass windows. Directly across and below sits the Catholic Church of the Immaculate Conception, overflowing on Sunday with devout Catholics from the village. This only served as a reminder of their differences.

Ireland had been through years of struggle, uprising and guerrilla warfare. In the years 1920–23 alone, the Irish Republican Party burned down 200 stately Anglo-Irish homes. In 1923, a group from the IRA had come to Glin with torches. The feisty twenty-seventh knight saved the castle. Although paralyzed by a stroke and wheelchair-bound, FitzJohn, as he was known, roared: "You'll have to burn me in it, boys!" driving them away. They never came back.

The newlyweds were a handsome couple. Desmond was lean and looked dapper in his tweeds. Veronica, now known as Madam FitzGerald, was strikingly beautiful, almost six feet tall and slender. Her son Desmond later wrote:

My mother was a tall, elegant woman with a straight nose and a fine oval face, she was a beauty. When she first married into Glin in 1929, the locals who were farmers to the man, loving cattle more than most, made the comment "ah sure, doesn't she have a fine fall for her water" which translated as "didn't she have a fine pair of long legs."

It cannot have been an easy existence. Despite the romance of living in a castle by the Shannon, the young bride found herself in a fairly isolated small Irish village, at least an hour and a half drive on potholed road to Limerick, the closest city. The winters were cold and rainy, with a constant wind off the Atlantic from September to March. The castle lacked central heating, electricity and indoor plumbing. Veronica would look out the castle windows to months of grey sky, drenched fields and a flat, grey river. Her father-in-law was reclusive, wheelchair-bound, cantankerous and depressed since the death of his young wife in 1901. Cared for by an unfriendly housekeeper named Sarah, he did not want change or innovation. Veronica's son Desmond wrote:

[the death of his wife Rachel broke]. . .the old knight's heart and he had become a virtual recluse only attended by his chauffeur/houseman, Jack, and a furious housekeeper, Sarah, who naturally deeply resented this new English broom trying to sweep through the dusty house.

The old knight sided with his loyal and familiar servant against the strong-willed newcomer and there were clearly plenty of battles. In his diary, Veronica's husband recorded many of the incidents:

AUGUST 22. THURSDAY 1929. GLIN. After the disgraceful & offensive way this foul old housemaid Sarah has behaved to Veronica, I think it is rotten of my father not to have given her notice at once. But the less said the better!!

NOVEMBER 18. TUES. 1930. GLIN. My father is being absolutely impossible & beastly to Veronica, so we have decided the only thing to do is keep away & take no notice of him. We motored into Limerick to do some shopping. . . .

Although they owned a castle and a 500 acre estate, the FitzGeralds were by no means rich. Money was relatively scarce during the Depression and wartime Ireland. But wealth is relative. While many Irish lived in squalor in unsanitary slums, the FitzGeralds man-

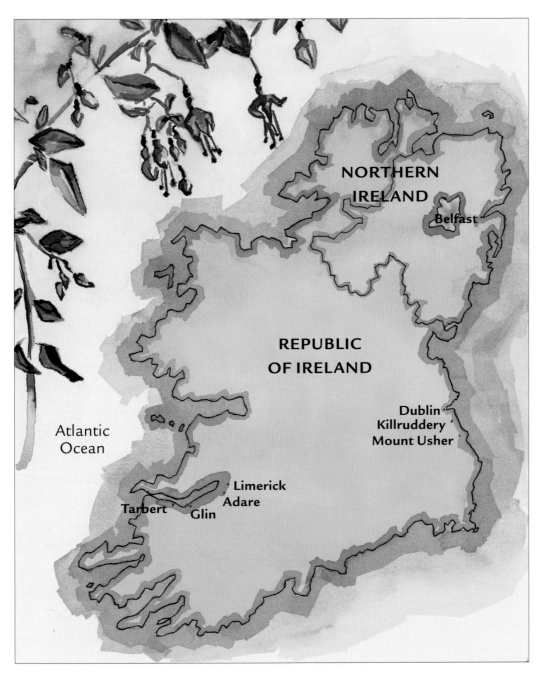

NORTHERN IRELAND

Belfast

REPUBLIC OF IRELAND

Atlantic Ocean

Dublin
Killruddery
Mount Usher

Limerick
Adare
Tarbert   Glin

Map of Ireland.

aged to maintain a flourishing social life. Each had a modest allowance. This meant they could still "do The Season" in Dublin
and London, and were able to travel abroad. A typical diary entry
of the time read:

JUNE 24. MON. 1929. LONDON. SAVOY HOTEL. *Left the
mail at Euston at 8 o'clock & went straight to the Savoy where
we are staying. We lunched at the Berkeley. Did a lot of shopping.
Dined early & went to see "Mozart" played by the Guitreys,
a splendid show.*

In October 1929, they took a six-year lease on a flat at 71 Park
Street, London, perhaps to escape the unpleasant domestic scene
with the old knight, but also to spend part of the year in the much
livelier cultural and social scene in London. The centre of their
lives, however, was in Ireland where they began to carve a life for
themselves. As his father was elderly and in ill health, Desmond
ran the farm and a salmon fishery. He oversaw the planting of
fields and vegetables, and ordered supplies and machinery for the
castle farm. He typically started tomato plants in the heated
glasshouse in January.

Desmond was described to me as a "very particular man." He
loved to sit in the warm spring sunshine and always insisted the
windows be kept clean, to let in the light. Veronica, meanwhile,
amused herself away from Glin. She was free to paint, pay social
calls or go shopping. She made weekly trips to Limerick with her
friend Eva, Countess of Dunraven.

Desmond and Veronica began to update the castle almost immediately after their marriage.

THURSDAY MARCH 28, 1929. *Have started straight away getting the house straight. The little sitting room which will be Veronica's we are starting on first.*

SUN MARCH 31, 1929. GLIN EASTER. *Busy deciding colour schemes & furnishing etc. for the bedrooms & drawingroom. We went to church in the afternoon. I have got landed to go on some church board or something.*

They purchased antiques, prints and watercolours for Glin. This was, no doubt, an astute decision as bargains were to be had from the estates of the declining Anglo-Irish. A great deal of furniture and art was apparently removed from grand old houses and sold to dealers by individual IRA members before the house was set on fire. As well, fleeing families readily sold art and paintings before their departure.

During Veronica's time in Ireland, the remaining aristocracy, or "Ascendancy," as they were called, were a small, tight-knit group. They struggled to keep up their stately homes and entertained one another at estates in a country that had little sympathy for their difficulties. Desmond and Veronica were constantly travelling between houses, attending lunches, hunts, horse shows and house parties. They made frequent shopping trips to Limerick. The Fitz-Geralds' friends were, for the most part, related to Desmond. Their friends were also considerably older, Victorian by birth and likely Victorian in their understanding of the world and their place in it. And, all of their close friends shared serious interests in gardens and gardening.

Desmond and Veronica's very good and close friend, Lord

Lord Dunraven at Adare. The Earl was a great friend of Veronica and Desmond.

Dunraven, was born in 1857. A colonel in the British army, he had
had a long military career and served in the Boer Wars. In 1885, he
married Eva Bourke, the daughter of the sixth Earl of Mayo and
served as military secretary to the Governor of Madras from 1886
to 1889. He inherited his title from his cousin in 1926.

Desmond and Veronica often stayed at Adare Manor with the
Dunravens and at Killruddery, near Dublin, the country estate of
the Earl and Countess of Meath. Desmond was a grandson of the
fourth Earl of Dunraven and Lady Meath was an aunt. Closer to
home, they visited their friends the Roycrofts, the Massys and

Aerial view of Adare Manor,
the country house of the Earl
and Countess of Dunraven.

Killruddery House and Gardens, the country estate of the Earl and Countess of Meath.

Cecil and Theodora (Theo) Leslie. The Leslies lived in an eighteenth century Georgian house in nearby Tarbert, County Kerry, close enough for tea or lunch after church or so that Veronica could, from time to time, ride on horseback to visit. Theo was also much older than Veronica. The estate had a huge red-brick walled garden and a park with clumps of trees across rolling fields; the riverbank had been cleared to reveal glimpses of the River Shannon creating a vision more perfect than nature. The walled garden, in typical fashion, was located down a meandering road, a distance from the house.

Adare Manor sat on a 1,000-acre park at the town of Adare, south of Limerick. The Gothic manor had no fewer than fifty-two chimneys and seventy-five fireplaces and a 132-foot long interior gallery with huge portraits. It was lit by heraldic stained-glass windows. According to writer Mark Bence-Jones, Lord Dunraven was passionate about trees and the estate had a huge collection of them; some had been planted over 300 years ago. In front of the

The gardens of Killruddery House.

manor were formal gardens laid out in a geometric pattern. Before dinner, a meal served by five footmen in moss-green livery, Lord Dunraven would take his numerous guests on long walks, teaching them the botanical names of trees and flowers. He was also a frequent visitor at Glin. One diary experts records the planting of an acorn tree that still flourishes in the garden:

> THURSDAY NOVEMBER 12, 1931: *Lord Dunraven came here in the morning with Allison his head gardener & gave me a lot of advise re trees & garden, etc. After lunch he planted the Killarney Oak grown from an "acorne"* [sic] *from the Killarney Oak at Adare.*

The rare and extensive baroque gardens at Killruddery, where Veronica and Desmond met and often visited, were laid out in 1682, a time in which the gentry were beginning to spend a great deal of money on extravagant gardens. Based on a design by Monsieur Bonet, the garden featured two 500-foot-long canals, a sylvan theatre, clipped hedges of lime, beech and yew and a feature known as the "angles," five avenues radiating from a circle in a *patte d'oie* design. These avenues were designed for riders or strollers to enjoy different views of the garden and surrounding Sugar-Loaf Mountains. The garden features several classical statues and fountains, great expanses of grasses, and, like Adare, a fine collection of trees. A Victorian conservatory was added in 1852. As garden writer Marianne Heron notes, "Gardening on this scale was not for those of slender means."

The original park at Glin was designed and laid out in the 1790s by James Bicknell, but the gardens gradually fell into disrepair until Lady Rachel Wyndham-Quin married the twenty-seventh knight

and moved to Glin in 1897. The layout at Glin is very formal near the castle, with clipped hedges. Beyond the castle, Lady Rachel planted informal fields with daffodils from the Scilly Isles. She and her husband also planted specimen trees that still stand today. Grass was allowed to grow long in the fields among daffodils, and around the trees. When Lady Rachel died in 1901, the garden was once again left unattended until Veronica arrived in 1929.

Like the renovations in the house, Veronica and Desmond became seriously interested in the castle garden very early in their marriage. Although Veronica always claimed that she restored the gardens at Glin, it is clear from his diaries that Desmond shared this interest and supervised much of the work. The gardens appear to have been a great source of pleasure and concern to him. He often recorded the progress of garden projects in his diary.

Desmond and Veronica planted trees and shrubs, including magnolias, dogwood and cherries. Veronica was especially fond of a Persian ironwood tree (*Parrotia persica*) that could be viewed from the castle. They cut down yew trees and pampas grass. The Pleasure Gardens were renewed with clipped hedges and formal walks. In the centre of the lawn, an eighteenth-century sundial was restored and became a favourite spot for family photographs. They built a rock wall that separates the formal from the informal gardens. Their friends probably encouraged their interests, and seemed happy to help the young couple.

Dunraven had a garden on Garinish Island that featured a large shrub and hydrangea collection. He gave the FitzGeralds many plants including peegee, lacecap, and blue hydrangeas from his extensive collection. The hydrangea border was completed in February 1940. Once established, the delicate blue flowers would often

On the grounds at Glin Castle.

win first prize at the August flower show in Limerick, where the FitzGeralds regularly exhibited. Dunraven also likely gave them specimens from his collection of trees. The Leslies gave a gift of camellias from their walled gardens. Before the war, the FitzGeralds planted Bay trees, a Christmas present from Desmond's aunt Nesta. Dick Charteris of Cahir Park, County Tipperary, supplied grape vines that were planted under protective glass. Others came to Glin with plants and advice until the garden was complete:

> TUESDAY. JANUARY 26, 1932. GLIN. *Still hard at work with the border in the garden, which is a very big one. Except for a collection of plants I bought from Holland we have been given everything by friends.*

Thus, much of their social lives revolved around the garden, and visits to gardens, and by other gardeners. Indeed, by the end of the Victorian era, "the garden had become the supreme symbol of the good life lived in the country" by the upper classes, Mark Girouard wrote in his study of *Life in the English Country House*. While attending their numerous house parties, they might spend an afternoon motoring along dusty and narrow roads to visit other gardens. One such garden was Abbeyleix, County Laois, noted for its large collection of fine trees and famous bluebell woodland. The Viscount deVesci and his wife, who Desmond described as "great gardeners," owned the Georgian house and estate.

As well as gardens, Desmond and Veronica shared a love of dogs. Desmond fondly remembered beloved Mogi, Sandy and Nigger (a name very common in the early part of the twentieth century) in his diary. Dogs were perennial fixtures in family

Garden at Glin with doves.

photos. Plaques on the inner castle courtyard wall marked their passing.

The amount of travel Desmond recorded in his diaries seems remarkable. At the time, roads were unpaved, narrow, winding and full of potholes. The road to Limerick had dangerous curves and narrow bridges. There were only two private cars in Glin during the 1920s, and the knight owned one of them. John O'Shaughnessy wrote that the village had no petrol pumps. Horses, donkeys and ponies were common and a daily bus service ran between Glin and Limerick. In his wonderfully descriptive book about travelling through Ireland in the late 1920s, writer H.V. Morton described a typical Irish town in which "cows come blundering through the street at all hours of the day; old men wearing decayed hats crouch on the shafts of donkey carts…"

Desmond at the
races in Dublin.

Morton also described the Irish railway system of the time this way: "Railway engines and carriages that would have been banished long ago by English public opinion still roll on over the main lines of Ireland and give to travel what Americans call an 'old-world air.' A trip to London meant car or bus, mail boat, the train to London and then, perhaps, a taxi. A weekend in Killruddery, south of Dublin, meant a trip by car, train and finally trap. Several diary entries suggest that the assistance of a chauffeur and/or maid were needed to transport the numerous pieces of luggage Desmond and Veronica would take with them.

Despite ongoing difficulty with the old knight, and Desmond's continued health problems, the marriage seems to have started off well enough. Veronica and Desmond clearly shared an interest in the garden, and continued to travel to Dublin, Limerick and London. They had picnics at the seashore at Ballybunion. Lunch parties, fishing and shooting, golf, weekend guests, horse shows and auto racing. Within a short time, the children came. Fiola was born in Dublin in the spring of 1930.

> 29 APRIL 1930. TUES. HATCH STREET. *Things started in the night. Dr. Salomons arrived at 8 o'clock in the morning. Frightfully worrying. A baby girl arrived at 9:20. Poor V. had a rotten time but it is over now. Saw her for a moment. I think very happy but not quite over the [event].*

After Fiola's birth, Desmond and Veronica vacationed in Jamaica. But they would not share many more months of happiness. Desmond had a premonition that 1932 would not be a good year. He wrote an ominous diary entry.

Veronica and Desmond
at Castle MacGarratt.

SAT JANUARY 2, 1932. GLIN. *Do not like the New Year starting
on a Friday. A bad omen, & is being already born out by my father's
behaviour. Busy in the office, gardener has done quite a lot since we
have been away.*

The year started without event, however, and life continued to re-
volve around trips to London and their close-knit circle of friends
and relations.

FRI APRIL 29 1932. LONDON. *We both had a busy day shopping.
Went to a cocktail party given by Elaine, & then dined with Helen
Adare & David Guthrie at "Quagling," (sic) went on to the "Café
de Paris" for supper and cabaret, & home again late as usual.*

47

Veronica became pregnant again in June. In the fall, they packed for their customary visit to Castle MacGarratt in County Mayo for grouse and pheasant hunting with Veronica's cousin. Desmond recorded that the baby was excited about her first major trip; he seemed to have no clue that marital bliss was about to come to a sudden end. Still deeply in love with his beautiful wife, he was devastated when, upon their arrival at the castle, he discovered that his marriage was dangerously threatened.

> OCTOBER 15 SAT. 1932. CASTLE MACGARRATT. *Serious trouble between Veronica & I & I am afraid it will lead to worse troubles...*

Veronica left for London, apparently with a lover. Much to Desmond's dismay, she did not write for an extended period of time. Desmond's diaries suggest that he became extremely depressed.

> NOVEMBER 8 TUESDAY 1932. *Left by morning boat & arrived Mayfair Hotel, London in the evening. Veronica met me. The most awful shock in my life, she no longer loves me. I feel that life is not worth living.*

> THURSDAY NOVEMBER 17, 1932. LONDON. *Veronica seems to have no sense of shame or decency. I can hardly believe it....*

Desmond seems to have had a very close relationship with Veronica's mother, Elaine, throughout his life. He often met with her in London to discuss the state of his marriage and to strategize about coping with his headstrong and apparently wayward wife.

MONDAY NOVEMBER 21, 1932 LONDON. *Lunched with Elaine*
& she told me the awful news of Veronica's character & the lies she
is telling. Elaine is all on my side & is rather a comfort to me. But
it is terrible.

Desmond came to be resigned to the situation, but never condoned it. He wrote, "The only way to have a married life without divorce is to give way.... I have done all I can. She has ruined my life and I hope will ruin her own..." Home life continued to be erratic and unhappy, chiefly because of Veronica's very frequent absences and reportedly objectionable behaviour. Divorce was not a desirable option in Ireland, even for Protestant families. It does not seem to be something Desmond would have sought in any event. They resumed life and they seemed to have, temporarily, reached an unhappy truce. He often described Veronica's behaviour as "impossible" and "inconsiderate." "Life," he wrote, was "hell."

On March 29, 1933, another daughter, Rachel, was born. This only added to Desmond's distress and disappointment. Not only was the child born amid great family discord, she was not the male heir they craved.

THURS. MARCH 30. 1933. WATERLOO PLACE. *Veronica &*
baby getting on well. Of course it is a terrible disappointment to us,
it not being a son. Sent wires off & notices in the papers.

Things were never the same after this and the FitzGeralds led increasingly separate lives. Veronica lived in a flat in London for a time, where she would meet Desmond for lunch on occasion. Despite the situation, Desmond wrote that he continued to love

Veronica. While in London in 1933, Veronica had a serious fall from a horse at Rotten Row, Hyde Park. She broke her leg and suffered a pelvic injury, which she felt, caused her many of the physical problems she had later in life. She told me about the incident years later. "What did I know at twenty four?" she mused. Desmond noted the fall in his diaries and expressed his concern.

TUES. NOVEMBER 14 1933. GLIN. *Rain at last, this has been the longest spell of fine weather I can remember. Planted the lavender hedge round the sundial. No letter from Veronica a damned shame, she knows I would be anxious about her fall.*

To an extent, Desmond began to resume the life he'd known before marriage. During this time, he discontinued keeping his detailed diaries, relying instead on pocket diaries. These contain the mundane details of daily life, such as shopping lists (film, hair oil, cigarettes, petrol, whiskey). He travelled to London, Madrid and Paris, the places he had known in his youth. Once, he noted that he gambled in the Casino Le Touquet until 7:30 a.m. He journeyed by sea to South America with friends in April 1934. He returned to Paris in 1935, attended the Brussels exhibition in June, and sailed to Oslo for a two-week cruise in July. He travelled to New York, Jamaica, Haiti, Peru and Chile in 1936. Photographs of mines, mine equipment and buildings in South America suggest that he may have been investigating investment interests. Veronica is noticeably absent from the photographs and diary from this period. Likewise, Veronica's photographs of Glin do not include Desmond.

On September 17, 1936, the old knight died. Presumably Desmond returned to Glin for the funeral and to assume the title of twenty-eighth Knight of Glin. With the death of Desmond's father, a significant source of friction between Desmond and Veronica ended. Perhaps hoping that their marriage might yet be salvaged, it appears they had a reconciliation at Glin. A photograph entitled "Family Group" was taken by the sundial in October with Veronica and Desmond together. That month, Veronica became pregnant once again. To her great delight, Desmond John, a son and heir, was born the following July. Desmond's journal entry for July 13, 1937 simply states: *"a son."*

Veronica planned to have the child in London so that he could claim British citizenship. She stayed with Desmond's aunt and then took a flat at 15 Cambridge Square, where Desmond was born. The plan was, however, "to no avail," she later told me. As an adult, Veronica's son Desmond has chosen to spend much of his life in Ireland. Nevertheless, the birth of a son and heir meant the title would carry on for another generation. It seemed to have had a beneficial impact on the marriage, and, perhaps, provided reason for Veronica to modify her behaviour. She and Desmond resumed married life, although it remained a marriage under considerable strain.

Veronica described the children's life at Glin during this time as idyllic. They had the castle gardens to frolic in, and each summer the family went on a seaside expedition to Ballybunion, near the mouth of the Shannon. The children built sandcastles near the steep Atlantic cliffs. At Christmas they decorated the castle with boughs of holly and ivy. Yet, family life was not quite as idyllic as Veronica portrayed. She could not have been an easy person to have as a mother and there was clearly still a great deal of tension in the household. A frequent visitor to Glin when the children

"Family Group" at the sun dial, Glin. October, 1936.

Desmond-John's
Christening,
September 1937.

were young, recalled that, whereas her husband spent his time in
the smoking room, the drawing room was Veronica's domain. Dinner at the long dining table was a stilted event with forced, uneasy
conversation. Desmond was sullen and withdrawn, while Veronica
attempted to keep up appearances.

Typical of aristocratic women of the time, Veronica was a less-
than-dedicated mother. While Desmond was trying to run the estate under what were to become extreme conditions, Veronica
seemed to spend an increasing amount of time away from Glin.
She was young and energetic, and refused to be confined to a
dreary, isolated castle with a sickly husband and small children.
Cooking, cleaning and other mundane chores were left to the servants. A nanny and governess cared for the children in the top-
floor nursery. Although she was the mother of three, Veronica told
me she had never bathed a baby. Children are "useless," she said,
until they are at least two years old. Her son Desmond described
his childhood in this way:

In the walled
garden at Glin.

*At teatime, heralded by the smell of a Balkan Sobrainie Turkish cigarette
appeared my mother. Tea and toast by the fire with my mother and Nanny
Reay were the high point of the day after disagreeable lessons from a primer
called Reading Without Tears (though there were many of them)! and other
educational efforts doomed, it seems to me, to failure. It was Una, the nursery maid and later the loyal family general factotum who really brought me
up and it was her quiet but firm influence which taught me to read, rite and
haltingly attempt 'rithmetic.*

So, the family struggled on. The children grew up in a picturesque
Irish castle beside the Shannon, with discontented parents engulfed in an unhappy marriage. There were, however, more difficulties to follow.

CHAPTER FOUR

The Darkest Years

Away with us, he's going,
The solemn-eyed;. . .
For he comes, the human child,
To the woods and waters wild,
With a fairy hand in hand,
For the world's more full of weeping
than he can understand.

— W.B. Yeats

WHILE LIFE WAS TENSE and difficult within the family, life in the outside world was also engulfed in trouble. For much of the 1930s, Britain and Ireland were involved in a trade war. Britain imposed enormous duties on agricultural products from Ireland, up to eighty-eight per cent on cattle. Ireland imposed retaliatory restrictions on imports of British goods, especially coal, cement, sugar, iron, steel and machinery. These restrictions served to compound the effects of the world-wide depression and would have had direct impact on a farm such as Glin. Much of the work was done by hand, with the help of donkeys, or horse and cart.

The trade situation with Britain improved, but unfortunately, more problems were on the horizon. First, while Desmond was supervising work on the farm and in the garden he was suffering from increasingly poor health. He often visited doctors, but could get little insight into his problems, which he most often referred to as the "flu."

FEBRUARY 16, 1939. THURS. GLIN. *Am only just beginning to feel fairly well again, it is extraordinary how long it takes to recover from this flu.*

He was put on an extremely restricted diet of four glasses of milk per day and told to reduce his cigarette consumption to three cigarettes per day. He noted he was "getting hungry already, 4 glasses of milk per day is not much to live on."

Then the war began. Ireland remained officially neutral during "the Emergency," as the war was called in Ireland. Desmond faced the possibility of military service. At first, he seemed excited at the prospect of serving Britain, and perhaps, in part, escaping his unhappy home life. He made enquiries about possible advantageous positions through friends and relations. He made several trips to Belfast and Dublin for medical examinations, but the reality of running the farm was an issue that could not easily be dismissed.

FEBRUARY 15, 1940. THU. GLIN. *Received my army calling up papers for next month. A hell of a blow with all this work here going on.*

He received a telegram stating, "Calling up indefinitely postponed." But, as he notes, he was "not off the hook." Finally, the matter was settled.

DECEMBER 17, 1940. TUES. BELFAST-DUBLIN. *Went before Medical Board at Victoria Barracks but they would not pass me due to recent illness, so that's that, I have done all I can. We returned to Dublin afternoon train, staying Kildare St. Club.*

As the war dragged on, transportation was disrupted and there were fuel shortages and food rationing. The Irish government instituted a policy of compulsory tillage for landowners.

Veronica and the children at Glin during the war years.

> JANUARY 25, 1941. SAT. GLIN. *The amount of land I have to plough up which is 12½% of the Demesne (arable) is 34 acres, a big undertaking.*

The amount required rapidly increased at the same time that supplies of petrol declined.

> JANUARY 3, 1941 FRI. GLIN. *Will have to plough up more land to comply with the emergency regulations, at lease another 10 acres in all.*

> FEBRUARY 4, 1941. TUES. GLIN. *Have at last received my special petrol allowance for tractor farm machinery etc. but instead of my previous 80 gallons per month now only get 20.*

As many young men, including Desmond's butler, enlisted in the army, there were difficulties getting help. He was often frustrated by the number of religious holy days when the men were not required to work. Furthermore, according to the diaries, Ireland was plagued with unusually bad weather during the war years. The winters were, he wrote, extremely harsh. At times, he spent his day huddled close to the fire worrying about the crops. The glasshouse had to be heated with wood rather than scarce coal, making raising tomatoes and other tender crops a more risky venture. Summers

brought abnormal periods of drought. In 1941, there was an outbreak of foot and mouth disease in Ireland.

APRIL 2, 1941. WED. GLIN. *Foot & Mouth Disease getting*
terribly serious, outbreaks all over the country, am sure it is being
spread by German agents.

Churchill tried to force Ireland out of her neutral position by imposing harsh import restrictions. The economy was once again
stagnant. Desmond purchased a tractor, but by 1942, the farm at
Glin was again using a horse and cart to gather hay, as there was little fuel. The FitzGeralds' social life was also severely restricted:

FEBRUARY 8, 1941. SAT. GLIN. *Veronica and I went up to*
Limerick by Bus the last run on this service owing to the petrol
situation. Returned loaded with shopping, etc. . .

Iris sibirica (Siberian flag)

The garden became vitally important during the war. The walled
kitchen garden at Glin contained vegetables, herbs, grapes, figs,
clematis and fruit trees espaliered against stone walls which moderate the worst effects of the wind and hold the heat of the day,
slowly releasing it in the night. For many years the garden provided
fruits and vegetables for the castle. Desmond began to investigate
alternative ways of keeping solvent. He looked at shifting the emphasis of the farm, their chief source of revenue.

JANUARY 8, 1942. GLIN. *Am trying to work out a scheme for the*
production of agricultural & vegetable seeds, usually imported &
now almost impossible to get. Think there might be something in it.

As well as producing seeds, the garden came to serve another purpose. Foynes is a small Irish village near Glin. From 1939–45, it became a vital aviation link to America. The first commercial passenger flight across the Atlantic left from Foynes on the Shannon River. Despite Ireland's neutral position in the war, top-level British and American military and diplomatic personnel used the base for high-priority flights to the United States, often using false passports. As well, famous politicians, businessmen, and even film stars used the route. Veronica often claimed that she came up with a plan to help in the war effort by selling crops from the large walled garden at Glin to the "flying boats" stationed at Foynes. Desmond was chiefly responsible for carrying out this activity. Due to petrol shortages, the crops were transported the nine miles to Foynes and back by donkey cart.

Rhododendron shilsonii
with seed head.

JANUARY 17, 1943. GLIN. *Sun. Have got a contract with British Overseas Airway to supply them with garden produce.*

AUGUST 8, 1943. SUN. GLIN. *Garden sales much better this year. Sullivan handed me £95 as against 69 last year.*

Dignitaries from Foynes were often guests at Glin, well before the contract to supply produce was signed. They would stay at the castle, coming and going on the trans-Atlantic flights. It is not clear from the diaries if these visitors were merely social, or if there was a financial transaction involved.

JUNE 2, 1941. MON. GLIN. *Capt. Stapleton. Chief Control Office of Foynes Air Port dined here.*

Garden at Glin.

APRIL 29, 1942. GLIN. Fiola's birthday. Harold Balfour, under secretary for air, & Sir Arthur Street came here in the evening & stayed for dinner. Harold is flying to America on special mission.

OCTOBER 7, 1944. SAT. Evans, head of Pan American Airways came to lunch, had long talk with him about passages on the Atlantic plane. Headford brought over several people including Gertrude Lawrence who are on their way to America. . . .

With the help of their many gardening friends and relations, work continued in the garden, despite the FitzGeralds' marital problems and the hardships of war. There was great excitement when Sir. Frederick Moore (1857–1949) and Lady Moore visited Glin in 1941. Moore was born at The Glasnevin National Botanic Garden, Dublin, where his father was director. He was appointed curator at Trinity College Botanic Garden in 1876 and upon his father's death in 1879, at the age of only twenty-two, Frederick became director at his father's Dublin garden. Moore became a noted garden expert. One of the original recipients of the RHS Victoria Medal of Honour and the Veitch Medal, he was knighted for his work in July 1911. He was known as the "Grand Old Man of Irish Horticulture."

Moore and his wife, Lady Phylis Moore, herself a knowledgeable plantswoman, often travelled to Irish gardens and enthusiastically shared their extensive knowledge of plants. During Moore's tenure at Glasnevin, new plant materials continually were being introduced from Asia, Australia, South America and other points around the world. The Moores distributed plant material, notably rhododendrons from the expeditions of plant hunters George Forrest and Frank Kingdon Ward, to gardens in which they felt they would flourish. Moore was eighty four years old when he visited Glin, and still actively involved in Irish garden circles.

Moore had been one of William Robinson's (1838–1935) closest friends. Robinson, famous for his advocacy of a natural style of garden, was in turn a friend of Gertrude Jekyll, the well-known garden writer associated with the Pre-Raphaelite movement of painters, poets and architects. Robinson's ideas of the natural garden were initially expressed in *The Wild Garden*, first published in 1870 and developed more fully in *The English Flower Garden* in 1883. He felt that only natural species should be used, and that the gardener should gather a range of exotic plants from other countries and arrange them in a manner suggesting they occurred naturally. Spreading garden meadows with colonies of bulbs and wild flowers, densely planted, were allowed to grow long, following the natural slope of the land.

As well as his association with the "wild garden," Robinson was considered a revolutionary in garden design. He was difficult and eccentric, however. No woman, for example, was allowed in his house. Even his good friend Gertrude Jekyll was served tea in the summer house. To say Robinson was outspoken would be an understatement. He carried on a fierce war of words attacking formal garden designs, characterizing their creators as villains. Frederick Moore, a man with a considerably more pleasing personality, was an active promoter of Robinson's ideas. He was especially instrumental in the development of the gardens at Mount Usher, south of Dublin, the Walpole family estate. Moore had first visited Mount Usher in 1885, shortly after Robinson visited the estate. E.H. Walpole wrote in 1929, "Many of the most valued specimens of the better and new plants at Mount Usher are there as a direct result of Sir Frederick Moore's interest."

Desmond enthusiastically recorded a visit by the Moores for several days to Glin in August 1941. Moore, known for his "magnetic" personality, seems to have strongly attracted both Desmond and Veronica. They arranged a large dinner party for their guests and even changed their prearranged plans, as they were so enthralled with all they were learning from their enchanting guests.

AUGUST 27, 1941. WED. GLIN. *We all went to the Limerick Horse Show, etc. very wet weather, but considering the times it went off quite well. Large dinner party here. Muskerrys, Moores, Justice Flood, Keating the Artist, etc. etc. etc.*

AUGUST 28, 1941. THURS. *We did not go to the 2nd day of the show; the Moores were far too interesting advising us over the garden etc. We got a 1st prize for the Hydrangeas yesterday.*

While Desmond struggled with farm management, Veronica developed an increasing interest in art. Like many artists before her, Veronica loved the stark beauty of western Ireland, including Connemara and the Aran Islands off Galway. She spent glorious hours painting this lonely, wild place, rocky and windswept by the thundering Atlantic. H.V. Morton described his 1930 travels through the West of Ireland in this way:

How can it exist in the modern world! In years of travel I have seen nothing like it. It begins suddenly as soon as you leave Galway due west by the coast road through Spiddal to Clifden. It is a part of the earth in which progress — whatever we mean by it — has broken in vain against grey walls; it has been arrested by high hills and deep lakes to the east and by the sea on the west. These people have been locked away for centuries by geography and poverty. I have been into the tomb of Tutankhamen in Egypt, but entering Connemara gave me a finer feeling of discovery and a greater sense of remoteness from modern life!

Veronica studied painting with Charles Lamb (1893–1965), a member of the Royal Hibernian Academy (RHA). In 1921, Lamb had visited the small village of Carraroe, in the Connemara Gaeltacht, and in 1935, he moved there permanently and built a house on the edge of town. There he started an annual summer school of art. Veronica often stayed with the Lambs and in June of 1941, despite the petrol shortage and restricted travel, she went to Carraroe and stayed for a month's painting course. When the weather was not too wet or cold, the young artists set off by bicycle with painting supplies as the sun rose over the unspoiled Atlantic coastline. Veronica and her artist friends would paint all day. At dusk, occurring late in the northern summer, the contented group would cycle home as the light changed colour in the western sky.

Veronica's artistic style expanded. She became a friend of Elizabeth Rivers, a member of the Society of Dublin Painters in the mid-1930s. This group formed in the 1920s in an effort to move away from the conservative RHA, which had historically ignored important modern movements such as Impressionism and the Pre-Raphaelite movement. Her circle of artist friends were well-educated, had private incomes and had trained on the continent.

Burren flowers.

She also came to know several artists associated with the Celtic Revival (or Irish Revival) movement. Veronica studied painting in Dublin and the diaries record an increasing number of artists and writers visiting Glin, many associated with the Celtic Revival. Charles Lamb (1893–1964), Sean O'Sullivan (1906–1964), Sean Keating, and W.B. Yeats' brother Jack formed a part of this flourishing group. Lamb and Keating were both students of William Orpen, one of Dublin's most celebrated painters. Veronica sat for a portrait with O'Sullivan. According to her son, this was not a success as the artist was mostly drunk while attempting to execute the painting!

Sean Keating was a frequent visitor at Glin, often staying several days at a time. He clearly became a part of Veronica's inner circle of friends. Keating, at one point president of the Royal Hibernian Academy, had been visiting and painting the west of Ireland as early as 1914. He learned the local Gaelic dialect, adapted the homespun clothing of the Aran Islands, and portrayed the local Irish Celtic fishermen and farmers in his paintings as heroic figures facing hardship with dignity.

Although mostly Protestant and Anglo-Irish, the Celtic Revival movement celebrated the rich traditions of Gaelic roots. The intellectual leaders of the Celtic Revival, most notably W.B. Yeats and George Russell (Æ) felt there were inherent differences between Celtic and Anglo-Saxon mentalities. Anglo-Saxons represented imperial domination, the scientific approach, materialism, industrialization and urbanization. The Celts, on the other hand, represented a culture that retained core values of the poetic, the heroic, the magical and the mythical. The Roman Empire, the Renaissance and the material domination of the Anglo-Saxon had not crushed them nor distorted their perception of life. The Irish and English, as a result, had inherent differences. O'Driscoll wrote:

The battle was not merely one of Ireland against England, not even one of people against people, but of the individual soul against bureaucracy, of spiritual forces against forces of empire and state, and a portion of the 'everlasting battle' between light and darkness, good and evil, spirit and matter.

The Irish Revival was interested in Celtic traditions and language. The painters of the Pre-Raphaelite movement influenced the members of the revival, just as they had influenced garden writers William Robinson and Gertrude Jekyll. In many ways, the Victorian "wild garden" and the Pre-Raphaelite movement had both been reactions against the commercialism and environmental destructiveness of the Industrial Revolution.

Veronica, unlike many of her friends and associates, was neither sympathetic to nationalist politics nor to Celts. She certainly accepted that the English and Irish were inherently different, but passionately disagreed about Celtic superiority. She no doubt had engaged in argument and discussion about the subject, and continued to do so throughout her life. These ideas were, and remained, core to Veronica's understanding of the world. She often told me that while the Celts were creative, they were not practical and "hopeless at organizing." It took, she said, an Anglo-Saxon to "get things done." Normans, her own ancestors, were, in her view, a combination of the best attributes of both Celts and Anglo-Saxons. She was, however, sympathetic to the movement's view on commercialism and, above all, clearly accepted the concept of the magical and of the existence of fairies.

Another important influence on Veronica was her acquaintance with the painter Augustus John. John and his family lived at Alderney Manor, a low pink stucco building in the Canford Estate, Veronica's grandmother's home. The tall, bearded Bohemian, like Veronica, abhorred commercialism and industrialism and had been influenced by the Pre-Raphaelites. Also, like Veronica, he often painted at Doolin, near the Burren in County Clare as well as at Connemara and Galway. Veronica claimed she had frequent contact with him. In Veronica's words, the swaggering figure "loved his drink and his women." He became a very popular artist and painted portraits of the Queen, George Bernard Shaw, Dylan Thomas, Tallulah Bankhead, and Lawrence of Arabia. He also made an oil sketch of Veronica's friend Mary Allington, a daughter of the ninth Earl of Shaftsbury. Until Veronica's death, a photo of this piece sat in the drawing room at Qualicum.

It is not known if Veronica met Yeats, as he lived much of his life away from Ireland and was in his declining years as Veronica came in touch with the group. He was, however, a member of the exclusive Kildare St. Club where the FitzGeralds often stayed. Furthermore, they knew some of the same people, including Augustus John. The FitzGeralds also attended performances at the Abbey Theatre in Dublin that Yeats had helped to establish.

One of Veronica's friends was Robert Gibbings (1889–1958). The son of a clergyman from Cork, Gibbings was an artist, book designer and travel writer. He, like others in Veronica's artistic circle, was an eccentric. For example, he went through a

Framed sketch of Mary Allington (right) by Augustus John in the Qualicum drawing room. A photo of Veronica's mother Elaine is on the left.

nudist phase, and would sometimes typeset in the nude. Gibbings had been neglected until recently. Many of his travel books, however, have been reprinted with his superb woodblock illustrations.

FEBRUARY 8, 1943, GLIN. *Robert Gibbings the well known Author and Artist came to stay for a few days.*

FEBRUARY 9, 1943 TUES. GLIN. *Took Gibbings over to Tarbert for tea with the Leslies. He is a most charming & terribly interesting man, in spite of beard & wide black hat!!*

During his stay at Glin, Gibbings showed both Veronica and Desmond how to divine for water, a skill that would prove to be of great benefit in the future. Desmond noted, "Strange to say we can both do it."

Veronica described some truly remarkable adventures experienced on her many visits to Western Ireland. Like many of the Irish writers of the early twentieth century, she was fascinated with tales of fairies. On one occasion, she told me that she and her friends took a native Irish currach to the Aran Islands. They planned to spend their time painting. Instead, the "king" of the Aran Islands greeted them and took them to a spot where the cold Atlantic is forced up through a blowhole for a spectacular display of nature's force. He then took them to a magical place where fairies lived.

She told an even more amazing story. The Burren is a wild, beautiful series of low, limestone hills in the northwest corner of County Clare. Subterranean streams, caverns and caves characterize the area. Rare alpine and Mediterranean flowers survive in

Sea Campion (*Silene maritima*).

crevices and fissures protected from cruel Atlantic winds. Warm Gulf Stream winds allow blue gentians, bloody cranesbills, ferns, honeysuckle and orchids to coexist. Scientists have found remnants of early habitation dating to the Bronze Age. The ruins of Celtic forts and churches dating to the twelfth century dot the area. Veronica claimed she and a friend saw the "little people" with their own eyes. She was convinced the original Irish still live underground in caves in the Burren!

Veronica carried on an extensive correspondence with an admirer, Sir John Randolph (Shane) Leslie, third Baronet of Glaslough, County Monaghan, which lasted for a number of years. Leslie was a prolific writer of poetry, novels, short stories, nonfiction and biographies. Like Veronica's mother Elaine, he was a cousin of Winston Churchill. He was considered a maverick and although he had written with great affection about his Anglo-Irish childhood, he became a Nationalist and a Roman Catholic. In 1916, he urged the British government not to carry out the execu-

The Burren in County Clare.

tions of those involved in the Easter Uprising. His quatrain in the Glin visitors' book, signed in both English and Gaelic, dated August 20, 1948, is typical:

> *He that would soul's peace and health of body win*
> *For he past gliding Shannon unto glamorous Glin!*
> *Still flies the flag of Desmond and poetic eyes can gleam*
> *Like shadow dancing stream and rule the ghost of Geraldine!*

Like so many of her friends, Leslie was interested in fairies and the supernatural. He wrote several ghost stories. In two of his many letters, he warned Veronica about his concern for her daughter Rachel. "Fairies will carry her away in a wild wisp of the wind to play fairy music to them." This would prove an unsettling prediction, as Rachel died of cancer as a relatively young woman.

After many years of ill health, Desmond was diagnosed with bovine tuberculosis, an epidemic rampant in the Limerick area. He received the bad news in June 1944.

JUNE 9, 1944. FRI. GLIN. *Veronica heard from Dr. Devane who has examined X Ray photographs with Dr. Abrahamson in Dublin. Afraid I have got Tuberculosis infection in lung. May have to go to Dublin later to have lung collapsed. I will be laid up for a very long time.*

Veronica told me she had read a magazine article about new treatments being developed for tuberculosis in America. In 1944–45, extensive research was being conducted at Rutgers University in New Jersey and at the Mayo Clinic in Minnesota. This research led to the development of streptomycin, an antibiotic used in the treatment of various bacterial infections, including tuberculosis. Veronica and Desmond would also have been well aware of the dude ranches and resorts of Arizona that specialists of the day considered a cure. These sanatoriums and dude ranches catered to wealthy Americans and Europeans.

Veronica arranged a flight to America for herself and Desmond with the help of her cousin, Lord Wimborne, the son of the former Viceroy to Ireland. Wartime flying was unpredictable and the trip took five days in windy weather. They flew from Foynes to Lisbon, then to the Portuguese Azores and finally across the Atlantic to Bermuda.

Veronica's unconventional Aunt Amy Guest had financed the trip and met them at two a.m. when they arrived in Florida. Amy had long loved airplanes and had planned to be the first woman to cross the Atlantic by airplane. In the 1920s, she had secretly acquired a Fokker 7 from Admiral Byrd, who had intended to use it on an expedition to Antarctica. Amy planned to use it to fly from America to Europe. When her family found out about her plans, they were fervently opposed to the idea and forbade it. Still wanting a woman to make the journey, Amy had her American lawyer find a suitable American woman to make the flight. She gave instructions that the woman "should be a pilot and well educated; preferably a college graduate. She should be physically attractive and have manners that would be acceptable to members of English society, who would undoubtedly welcome her on her arrival…" Amelia Earhart made the trip, financed by Aunt Amy, on June 17, 1928.

When Desmond and Veronica travelled to America at Amy's expense, Desmond was very ill and had been so for some time. It must have been an extremely difficult trip for him. Tuberculosis is characterized by cough, pallor, night sweats and advancing weakness. Desmond's notes suggest that things did not go well with Aunt Amy, whom he describes as "quite mad." Amy was apparently distressed that Veronica and Desmond were not willing to "stay with her in all parts of the USA…for her advertisement and convenience…" She became, he wrote, "more than nasty."

As winter approached, the FitzGeralds travelled to New York and Chicago, where Desmond saw a series of doctors. At the end of November, they headed to Arizona for the winter. Fighting in Europe had continued through the summer and fall of 1944, and Desmond wrote that the train they boarded was full of injured soldiers in beds and carriages, as American wounded were returning home from the war. There were long waits for the dining car and, Desmond noted, they lined up for over an hour to eat. On the train, they met the Canadian businessman Ray Milner and discovered they knew someone in common, perhaps a relation of Ray's Irish wife, Rina.

Veronica's desert painting,
now at Glin Castle.

NOVEMBER 29, 1944. WED. *We left New York by train at 4:15.*
Have a comfortable drawing room. Met a very nice Canadian called
Milner who we saved for dinner.

NOVEMBER 30, 1944. THUR. *Arrived Chicago about 9 a.m.*
Went Palmer House Hotel, one of the biggest in the world. Snowing.
Milner lunched with us. Left 8:30 pm for Tucson, Arizona.

Perhaps it was at the Palmer House Hotel where an incident
Veronica described to a friend took place. The FitzGeralds arrived
in a grand hotel in a large American city and Desmond signed the
hotel register in their proper names: The Knight of Glin and
Madam FitzGerald, as Irish hereditary knights are not referred to
as "Sir" and "Lady," in the manner of knights titled by the current
monarch. Desmond was taken aside by the hotel manager who

said, "I'm sorry. We can't accommodate you." The embarrassed manager explained the problem. This was a high-class hotel and the gentleman and his companion were not welcome, as they were obviously not married.

When they arrived in Arizona, they settled in a "dude ranch" which was crowded and unpleasant. Desmond consistently referred to the owners as "crooks." He was especially critical of "Mrs. R." whom, he wrote, is "not only common but bloody." At one point, they were asked to leave the facility, as Veronica was involved in what Desmond described as "a real feud." Things seemed to improve when they moved to Mrs. Carr's ranch near Tucson. Desmond was likely under the rigorous rules typical of sanatoriums of the day. Patients followed a strict routine of early rising, early retiring, moderate activity, fresh air and good food. Some experts insisted on absolute silence during long rest periods.

While Desmond lay in the infirmary, Veronica enjoyed the desert. As an artist, the cloudless sky and the changing colours of the day captivated her. The sky is big in the southwest, horizon to horizon, with no canopy of trees or clouds to block the sky. At night, only the light of the moon inhibits the stars. Shadows follow you across the land. The sun paints mountains red in the evening; the morning light in winter looks like frost on the cactus. As a naturalist, she would have been enchanted with quail, Audubon's warblers, sparrows, gilded finches and woodpeckers. Veronica attended what must have seemed primitive barbecues over open fires. She painted and photographed desert plants: yucca, cholla, saguaro and barrel cactus.

As a health cure, however, it had not been a successful trip. Relieved to be home in rainy Ireland, Desmond wrote:

Veronica painting in the desert near Tucson, Arizona.

*Veronica and myself had a very difficult time and instead of im-
proving in health in that wonderful Arizona sun it was all wasted
and thank God I am once again back in my own home. Although
the damp country may not be the best I feel more happy.*

The war ended and while much of the Western world enjoyed an
economic boom, Ireland's economy remained stagnant. The country remained isolated and conservative. Desmond, meanwhile,
remained ill. He began to complain about Veronica's behaviour
again, a theme which would prevail for the rest of his life.

JUNE 9, 1946. SAT. GLIN. *Stayed in ill all day feel far
from well, & Veronica is not helping by being so
unpleasant. What a life.*

Yet, he was not unsympathetic to her. As his health
grew worse, Veronica was forced to take over many of
his duties in running the estate.

OCTOBER 26, 1946. FRI. GLIN. *Poor Veronica is
becoming* really worn out *trying to run the house & do
all my estate management as well. If only I could get up.*

Around this time, Shane Leslie wrote long and highly poetic let-
ters to Veronica. He seemed to be infatuated with her great beauty.
He opened one letter with, "And how are you, beauty of the rocks
and queen of the hills – ?" In another, he praised the
*Lady of Glynn
Whom the Bards have sung in prophecies ecstatic for three centuries:*

white rose of the rocks of Kerry:
lithe hazel-rod of the fairy men.

While Desmond was ill, Leslie seemed interested in assisting with young Desmond's education and even acted as a tutor to the boy for a time. He also shared an interest in trees and from July 17 to 25, 1948, chaired a forestry conference in Dublin, which was to include excursions into the mountains, meetings and the planting of several trees in Dublin's 1,753-acre Phoenix Park. He wrote that he would like to visit with Veronica, even though "I shall be like a raging lion and a crushed umbrella alternatively during the forestry week but I hope to survive." He hoped his efforts would cause both the Irish press and government to appreciate the importance of forestry in Ireland. "Trees, trees, trees — we must plant them by the million or our diminishing millions of populace will die off the land. I hope you won't mind an insane silviculturalist in the house," he wrote.

Desmond had a lingering and painful death. He appears to have rallied for a time and they travelled to England and then to Monte Carlo. In Monte Carlo, the situation took a turn for the worse as his disease advanced.

MARCH 5, 1947. WED. MONTE CARLO. *Very bad X ray report. Trouble in both lungs now. Must go to Switzerland as soon as possible.*

Desmond spent over a year in sanatoriums in Switzerland. He spent an extremely unhappy time and complained of the "shocking" food and uncaring help and various "scandals" in the institutions. He wrote: "How I wish I could lend a bit of a hand with everything and at the same time have a really comfortable bed and none of the noise and racket that goes on here and O! to hear English or even Irish spoken once again." At one point, Veronica joined him, and took short trips through Switzerland, Rome and Florence with their daughter Fiola.

Remarkably, Desmond continued to make journal entries almost until the end, often expressing great distress at his relationship with Veronica and what he regarded as her extremely self-centred behaviour. He seemed to have expectations about the role of a wife that Veronica was unwilling or unable to meet. On occasion, he refers to love affairs she was having.

JAN. 1, 1948, THUR. MONTANA HALL. *The start of another year, probably my last. I wonder if the day after day hell of last year is to continue through this!? Things would be more bearable if Veronica was only behaving like a loyal and kind wife. But she has no feeling & only thinks of herself. A nice entry for a New Year.*

SEPTEMBER 2, 1948. FRI. GLIN. *Veronica is nagging and cursing me day and night, O God I do hope I will die soon.*

Veronica's mother, Elaine, seems to have stayed at Glin a great deal during the period when Desmond's health was in serious decline. She is pictured in the garden with the children. Elaine's presence left Veronica free to run the estate, or pursue her various interests. It also left her free to travel, which seems to have been a relief to Desmond.

Veronica's mother stayed at Glin while Desmond's health declined.

MARCH 3, 1949. THURS. GLIN. *The little peace of mind I have been having for the last week or so, ended now that V. is back. Very stormy and cold. In bad pain in chest. Can hardly move.*

The FitzGeralds had many loyal and lifelong staff in Ireland. In some cases, the families had been employed at the castle over several generations. The Healy family was such a family. Paddy Healy was born the same year as Desmond and came to work with his father at Glin at age eight. The two boys grew up together and became good friends. The Friday before he died, Desmond called maid Nancy Ellis up to his room. "Ring Paddy Healy for me." He and Paddy sat by the glass door, perhaps in soft spring sunlight, and made plans for Desmond's funeral.

Desmond died on April 2,1949 at Glin and is buried in the small ancestral churchyard at the gates of the castle. His tombstone erroneously records his death as April 2, 1948.

Nancy recalled that the knight died at about five a. m. Veronica stood in the kitchen looking out the window. "He's gone," she said, "there's two of me now." After Desmond's death, Veronica was left a single parent in Ireland with an unprofitable estate and three children, but little money to support either the estate or herself and the children. In her forties, she was still a very attractive woman. She had to make ends meet with no particular skills, a circle of well-off and well-connected friends and relations and her indomitable willpower. Post-war Ireland continued to be gloomy. A stagnant economy, a conservative government and church kept the country archaic and secluded. She raised chickens, continued to sell vegetables, sold her desert paintings and even took in paying guests.

Desmond was buried in the ancestral church yard near Glin. His tombstone erroneously records his death as April 2, 1948.

IN LOVING MEMORY OF
DESMOND WINDHAM OTHO FITZ-GERALD
28TH KNIGHT OF GLIN.
BORN 20TH JAN. 1901
DIED 2ND APRIL 1948.

Veronica, however, was determined to endure, no matter how impossible the idea seemed. Although she had often complained about the loneliness and isolation of Glin, family pride and perhaps, a desire to see her son assume the hereditary title of "Knight of Glin," made Veronica determined to save it. Her son recalled: "I always remember how furious she was when Aileen Meath, my father's aunt, called Glin a white elephant." It was hard to manage, but I am again reminded of one of Veronica's expressions, "It's not for nothing that I'm a Churchill." Leaving Ireland for her family in England was probably an option. In 1953, Veronica stayed for a time in London. Her mother urged her to consider selling Glin. "I know it would be sacrificing family pride…to part with Glin but you & the girls would not be so harassed on a larger income [instead on concentrating on] farming unknown and unliked by you," she wrote.

It was a difficult time. Veronica, Nancy recalled, weeded the garden and pruned roses herself in the evenings. Rachel and Fiola picked and bundled daffodils to be sold at the market in Limerick. Nancy churned butter by hand in the castle kitchen. It, too, was potted and weighed for sale. Two pigs were fattened, one "for sale" and the other "for bacon." One year, Nancy recalled, Veronica made £300 from the chickens she kept. There was even a great deal of strife among the staff. Nancy recalled the friction. There was a "murderous cook" who would not get up until eight in the morning. Nancy and Una, however, got up at six a.m. to begin the day's chores, including lighting the fires in the unheated castle. One day, someone stole the cook's tea and he complained bitterly to Veronica. "We admitted to it right away," explained Nancy. The tea was kept in a locked cabinet and the women could not have a cup of tea to take off the morning chill until the cook got up. Veronica settled the matter by arranging for the women to have their own shelf stocked with tea and bread.

Veronica had at least two suitors during these years, so marriage may have been a possibility. Her personal maid and confidante, Una Bourke, forwarded a letter from one of them with the following caution:

I sent on a letter to you from Sir H. and I saw by the Post mark that he is still in Spain. . .to tell you the truth I don't have a very happy feeling about it, but for your sake, I hope its alright, if you haven't by now learnt different. Madam I do still *think you are much too good for him, so if it does fall through, which to me it seemed to be doing* Don't Worry, "God" *has something much better in store for you. If on the other hand, it does come to something I should strongly advise you to stand firmly, and make him feel that "Woman is PRIDE" and you must be treated accordingly without any other influences, otherwise you will be lost, as I'm afraid he would always want a certain amount of freedom, which would not be a happy existence for you, and you would be so miserable, and so would I.*

As she struggled to keep the castle and estate intact during this uncertain time, Veronica began what would later become an obsession. In February 1953, she enlisted the help of friends and politicians whom she felt would be of some influence in forming a "National Trust for Ireland." This would be based on the National Trust for England, Wales and Northern Ireland, which was founded in 1895 to protect places of natural beauty or historic interest. She wrote to the famous Irish photographer, Father Browne, whom she hoped would devote his "great cultural, historical & architectural knowledge on our behalf." Browne, a Jesuit priest and classmate of James Joyce, was from a prominent Cork family. He had been documenting social, religious and commercial life in Ireland throughout his life. He became famous for his photographs of the *Titanic* and for his efforts to have photography recognized as an art form. Shane Leslie introduced Veronica to Father Browne who both photographed and wrote an article on Glin in 1950. Veronica wrote to Father Browne:

It occurs to me that you of all people would be the greatest possible help to the furtherance of keeping up the beautiful & historic houses in this country...

In 1951, Veronica commissioned a rather extensive horoscope by an unknown astrologer. According to this document, the stars dictated that Veronica was a person possessing "a basic individualism and independence...a practical idealist." Her sun sign of Aquarius gave her artistic and creative abilities, perhaps an interest in landscape architecture. The stars also dictated that Veronica would be "sensitive, nervous, rather highly strung" and have "some measure of perversity, erratically [sic], dislike of convention and control." Although in possession of "an exceptionally alert and active intellect," she lacked "warm-heartedness."

The astrologer predicted Veronica would marry more than once, likely to a person considerably older than herself. She would have a trip abroad and the horoscope concluded, "You will have a year of marked good fortune in business and money matters during 1954." She would begin to enjoy herself and have more time for leisure pursuits, the astrologer went on to write. "You will find that others tend to be particularly kindly and considerate... In particular one would say that there is a probability of an old friendship being rather happily renewed." The astrologer declared that Veronica was at a crossroads in life and, once again, that the year 1954 would be "distinctly fortunate from the business, domestic and family aspect."

CHAPTER FIVE

Ray Milner

Thine ancient trails and tangled maze,
With garlands fair arrest my gaze;
Cool leafy bank and mossy dell,
Unite thy pleasing charms to tell.
Thou source of ever-flowing streams;
Thy underlying mineral seams,
And wealth in wood and water-power,
Great benefactions on us shower.

—C.E. Lund

Y ALL ACCOUNTS, Ray Milner was a wonderful man: strong but compassionate, sophisticated but with a "down eastern" homeliness. He had good taste and a sense of humour. He collected fine art and books, but also loved detective stories. Over time, Ray became an accomplished and influential Canadian. He sat on the board of over twenty Canadian companies including the Royal Bank, Canada Cement Company, North American Life Assurance, and Burns and Company. He was senior law partner in the firm of Milner, Steer, Dyde, Massie, Layton, Cregan and MacDonnell. Despite his many accomplishments, Ray Milner has largely remained out of the history books, preferring to work quietly and efficiently behind the scenes.

Ray Milner was born in Sackville, New Brunswick in 1889, from a distinguished United Empire Loyalist family. The son of William C. Milner, L.L.D. and Althea Smith Milner, he graduated from King's University in 1909 with a B.A., the same year that Veronica was born in London. He continued his education and graduated from Dalhousie University in 1911 with a law degree. One of his professors was Sir Robert Borden, a successful Halifax lawyer who was soon to become Conservative Prime Minister of Canada.

Ray was called to the bar in 1911, but job opportunities for young lawyers in the Canadian Maritimes were not plentiful. Ray had few prospects and a chronic bronchial condition. His abrasive Aunt Sarah Ketchum offered some blunt advice: "Go west." She gave him $500 to start him on his way.

The West was booming. In Edmonton, the rhythm of hammers announced the building of housing tracts, packing houses and streetcar lines. In the rural areas, other newcomers settled, drawn by the promise of free or inexpensive farmland when Alberta became a Canadian province in 1905. The number of Alberta acres planted with wheat increased from 271,000 in 1908 to 879,800 in 1910. Between 1901 and 1911, its population increased from 73,000 to 374,000. The transcontinental railway ran through Edmonton, and marked the starting point to the gold fields of the north, adding to the frontier excitement of the expanding town.

Ray arrived in Edmonton in 1912 with $75 in his pocket. He, along with many other young men, stayed in the "Victoria Estates," a transient tent town set up on the north side of Victoria Road. "There were no sidewalks and the mud was mighty deep," Ray recalled of Edmonton in the early days. He lived in primitive, uncomfortable circumstances, until the brutal northern winter forced him indoors.

About this time, Ray met and was attracted to a much older woman, Mrs. Catherine Bury. The 1912 edition of *Burke's Landed*

Gentry of Ireland notes that Catherine (Rina), daughter of Maurice Collins, Shauntrade, County Limerick, had married William Pennefather Bury of Little Island and Curraghbridge, in 1899. They had three children. Now separated, Rina had just arrived in Canada from County Limerick, Ireland. A photograph shows an attractive woman with large, soft eyes. Her curly, dark hair is brushed away from her face. Much later, Ray described her as "very fine looking & tho' high tempered was goodhearted, kind & loyal."

When the Great War broke out, Ray joined the Edmonton Fusiliers as captain and adjutant. He pursued a military career despite health problems and poor eyesight, apparently memorizing the eye chart to pass the army fitness tests, which would have otherwise disqualified him. Alberta had one of the highest enlistment rates in Canada during the war. At one point, men queued outside the armouries to sign up, motivated by both patriotism and the harsh circumstances of their lives. Ray explained: "No one had any concept of what war would be like. Some men walked 250 miles from the north country to join but times were tough and three squares a day and clothes looked pretty good." Canadian historian Howard Palmer describes the hasty departure of one young homesteader and his brother from the Peace River region of northern Alberta. They left a note tacked to the door of their shack: "War is hell, but what is homesteading?"

Ray's battalion was not called into active duty. Determined to go overseas, he reverted to the rank of lieutenant and on October 13, 1916, he sailed to Europe on the SS *Olympic* with the 26th Infantry Battalion of the Canadian Second Division. He had six extra pairs of glasses hidden in his bag!

Ray arrived in England on October 20, 1916, and at Bramshot

Ray Milner in the Great War.

Rina Milner.

was posted to the Canadian Forestry Corps. He served in the trenches in France, and on March 30, 1918 was wounded. The wound was treated and recorded but was minor, and Ray remained on duty. On May 5, 1918, near Rouen, the misery and terror of the trenches ended for Ray. Shrapnel blasted his hand, right calf and neck. That day, Ray was treated in the Number Two Red Cross hospital. Later, the end of his left thumb was amputated and he was evacuated to the hospital at Reading, England. On June 29, he was sent to the Canadian Convalescent Officers' Hospital at Matlock Bath, Derbyshire. There, Ray's old bronchial problems flared up. He began to spit up blood and developed pains in his chest. He was tested, and cleared for tuberculosis. These injuries and his subsequent hospitalisation proved to be not entirely unfortunate. Years later, Ray told a reporter he was "glad to get out of those trenches." But there was another reason the situation was fortunate for Ray. By marvellous coincidence, Rina Bury, the woman whom he had met and admired in Edmonton, had also joined the war effort and was nursing in England where they met again.

Ray was "struck off the strength," as a result of the general demobilization on April 3, 1919. He married Rina and in 1921, at age thirty-two, he was named King's Counsel. He became involved with utility companies as legal counsel in 1923 and acted as personal counsel to Canadian Prime Minister R.B. Bennett. In 1931, Ray travelled to London and argued before the Privy Counsel on behalf of the province of Saskatchewan, one of only a few Canadian lawyers ever to argue before the highest court of appeal. In 1932, he became president of Northwestern Utilities, Canadian Western and Canadian Utilities Limited.

When he retired, a reporter asked Ray what accomplishment in his career gave him the most satisfaction. "Well," he said, "I think taking over two technically bankrupt companies in 1932, fighting through the Depression, getting them on their feet where today they are very wealthy, is my greatest pride. I went to bed facing bankruptcy and I got up in the morning facing bankruptcy."

Despite his achievements, Ray Milner never seemed to forget the struggles he had as a young man and the lessons he had learned in the war. During the Depression years, war veterans, alcoholics, the hungry and penniless were not turned away from the Milner door. Ray apparently had the empathy to understand what might have led a man to this state. The St. John's *Edmonton Report* noted that neighbours recalled a "steady stream of people to his doorstep" at the big house at 11618–100 Avenue in Edmonton. One of his acquaintances told me Ray was "generosity itself," and many others have described specific acts of kindness or charity. Ray's generous nature was demonstrated in a more formal way by his service to a number of organizations including the Edmonton Community Chest, the YMCA, the Canadian National Institute for the Blind, the Canadian Arthritis and Rheumatism Society and the Canadian Welfare Council, among others. He is especially remembered for many years of devoted service to the Salvation Army.

With his triumphs in business, Ray and Rina began to search for a summer getaway. Several businessmen from Edmonton had summer houses in Qualicum Beach, on the east coast of Vancouver Island. By now, they had a daughter who had had polio, and it was thought that the coastal climate would be good for her. The town had a long British tradition, a good highway for easy access and a moderate climate.

In 1937, the Milners travelled to the Island and met with a colourful local enterpriser, General Money, at Money's Qualicum Beach house. Noel Money was born in Montreal in 1867 and educated in England. His father had served in India during the mutiny of the spring of 1857, when a number of British women and children were massacred. Like his father, Money served in India. He landed in Bombay in 1889, a member of the Royal Irish Fusiliers. He served during the Boer War and was awarded the Queen's South Africa medal.

Money came to Vancouver Island on a fishing trip in 1913, bought several lots and moved his family to Qualicum Beach. At the outbreak of the Great War, he returned to Britain to resume his military career, becoming something of a hero. He commanded the 159th Brigade, Welsh Division, during the capture of the Mount of Olives, Jerusalem, in 1917. After his distinguished military career, Money returned to Qualicum in 1919. In many ways, Money put Qualicum Beach on the map when he opened the Qualicum Hotel. It was a huge success and attracted the rich and famous from around the world during its heyday from the 1920s to the 1940s. Some of those who stayed at Money's hotel included Edgar Rice Burroughs, Errol Flynn, Bob Hope, Bing Crosby, Shirley Temple and even the king of Siam.

Money's sister, Hilda Bayley, and mother, Emily Louisa Money, moved to Qualicum Beach in 1929 and began to build a large cottage, which was completed in 1931. A.N. (Alex) Fraser signed the original drawing for the house entitled "Cottage for Mrs. Bayley." Fraser owned Qualicum Construction and was the premier builder in the area. The undated plans show that both the large bedroom and the "pink" room could access the "sun room" at the western end of the house. This was later closed off so that access was exclusively from the large bedroom. A dining room, kitchen, drawing room, spare bedroom (the "yellow room") and a small "maid's bedroom" completed the cottage. During the Depression, the company kept several local men employed part-time working on this and a neighbouring house.

The Bayley family owned a tea plantation in the colony of Ceylon, now Sri Lanka. The Qualicum cottage was built to include features of a Ceylonese tea plantation house, reminiscent of the family's time in the hot, humid colony. During the Raj, bungalows (from the Hindustani word *bangla* meaning "from Bengal") were built to withstand both monsoon rains and hot sun. Eaves, spreading from the roof, gave protection from rain in the monsoon climate of India and Ceylon. Each bungalow had a veranda. In Ceylon, the veranda typically became a cool outdoor room complete with potted plants, blinds and cane furniture. Thus, at Qualicum, tea and cocktails were served on the veranda or in the garden.

Each bedroom had its own bathroom. This was highly unusual in a Canadian house in 1929, but very common in the British houses of Ceylon. Screened doors to the outside were built in each bedroom. In India and Ceylon, this served to provide additional ventilation and allowed servants to clean up or draw a bath without disturbing the occupants of the room. At Qualicum, the set-up also allowed privacy and easy access to the grounds for guests and family.

Due to Mrs. Money's ill health, the Bayley family only lived in the house for a short time. When the Milners visited Qualicum, the estate was for sale. After lunch with Money, the Milners proceeded to the estate, a short distance away. They drove down the

The house – early photo, circa 1931.

long driveway, through the cool, dark forest. Cedars and Douglas-firs rose above salal, huckleberries and ferns. They reached the clearing and a stunning blaze of early spring flowers in the garden. The slap of waves and the scent of salt revealed that the sea was not far away. The beauty of the place captivated them and on April 14, 1937, they bought the property in the name of Catherine Milner.

The Milner family used the house primarily in the summer, but were known to spend a short time in the spring, and sometimes Thanksgivings, at Qualicum. Rina spent more time at Qualicum than Ray, who was often busy with his many business and legal affairs. It was Rina's house. She established a warm and welcoming haven for family and friends, where laughter flowed. Both Ray and Rina loved to entertain and guests loved to be entertained by the couple. They extended their hospitality to Ray's business associates.

Early photographs show extensive clearing in the trees. The

garden, especially near the house began to take shape: the circular driveway around a chestnut tree, an orchard and flower beds near the house. Years later, Veronica told me that several trees, including the Red May or hawthorn trees, were "planted by Mrs. Money." We quickly came to realize this really meant "planted by Rina Milner."

Ray and Rina both took an active role in the garden, and both loved the forest. Rina especially loved the trees. Like Ray, Rina had a great reluctance to cut any down. Rina also loved roses and hydrangeas, and planted many near the house. Her efforts at gardening were hampered, however, by severe water problems. Water was stored in holding tanks on the property. At night, she would send her daughter out to turn the sprinklers on, much to the caretaker's dismay. He would turn the water off. Rina would again send her daughter out to turn the water on.

The children and grandchildren would play on the grass, in the forest, or run on paths along the clifftop. A cast bronze bell with a bracket, which still stands outside the sunroom, was purchased for $10 and used to summon the family for dinner. The atmosphere was free, open and informal. On warm nights, the children slept in the sunroom or in a tent nearby, while the sound of laughter mingled with the smell of cigar smoke and drifted in the air. A brass box sat on the veranda full of sandals, as much time was spent on the beach. A grandson recalled: "Sand was everywhere!"

Despite a very busy life, Ray or his secretary Miss Chisholm always took the time to write monthly letters to the caretaker, Robert Strouts, and his wife at Qualicum. The Stroutses would prepare the home for the family. The letters hint at Ray's life of constant travel: San Francisco, Ottawa, New York, Montreal, London and Vancouver. Ray had an office in Edmonton and another in Calgary. In 1942, he was joint chairman of the National Progressive Conservative convention. He ran for office as the Conservative candidate in Edmonton-West in the 1949 federal election, but lost by 6000 votes to the Liberal candidate as the St. Laurent Liberals won a landslide election. Around this time, Ray sent the following hurried instructions for planting the garden:

Consider the following:

Hollyhocks behind new hedge

Gladiolae in garden

Creeping roses against garage where peach tree stood

If pansies do not need much sun — in bed at back of home

Move hydrangeas now at back of house to bed along road or near it

Move tall yellow flowers now in bed along road to edge of trees

Concentrate different kinds of flowers as much as possible

North side of lawn going west

No. 1 bed (running beside trees) — Generally poppies. Will buy in spring some California tree poppies

No. 2 bed — Flox-will buy 6 in spring

No. 3 bed — Only roses — two or three more

No. 4 — Marigolds (as is)

No. 5 — Tulips and when they are through, then genias — no border

Front of house — North to South

No. 1 — Flagstones

No. 2, 3 & 4 (24 yards) — Holland Dahlias to be purchased from Highland Barnes.

In the spring of 1947, Ray and Rina travelled to London and Ireland via New York. This was an unusual trip as Rina had been in poor health for several years, and so did not often accompany Ray on his travels. Perhaps she knew how ill she was and wanted to see her children and grandchildren one last time. It appears the Milners also visited Rina's native soil in County Limerick, Ireland. Ray, and his stepson Phineas Bury, also visited Glin Castle before returning home.

The area around Qualicum was becoming increasingly attractive as a retirement community. It had always been of interest to those of British extraction and had even seen its share of royalty. In 1919, the Prince of Wales visited officers convalescing in Qualicum Beach. In 1951, Princess Elizabeth and the Duke of Edinburgh visited the area on their extended trip across Canada and stayed at the Eaglecrest Lodge, very near to the Milners. Similar to Victoria, Qualicum Beach was very English. Qualicum was an oasis of "civility." Not only sheltered from the wind and rain by Mount Arrowsmith, it was cocooned from the more rugged aspects of Island life.

Qualicum was also the retirement centre for a large number of British remittance and military men. One of the Milners' adjoining neighbours was the appropriately named Major Archibald Cross. Cross was described to me as a "difficult, unpleasant" man who had a particular hatred of women. Cross bunkered himself in his small cottage, buffered from real or imagined foes with a double fence, topped with barbed wire. His caustic tongue was like a steely weapon. Cross himself seems to have had at least some insight into his unpleasant nature, perhaps heightened as his own

Winter at Qualicum
in the early years.

health began to fail. He also appears to have had a special regard for Rina.

Rina had long suffered from a hereditary illness and for twelve years she had been in increasingly poor health. Major Cross wrote a series of letters to Ray from the Guards Club, Berkley Square, London and from Qualicum. In one he wrote, "I am worried about her [Rina] being sick, as my conscience tells me I have been rather rude to her in the past years as she used to kindly ask me to feed with you both on numerous occasions. I do know she is the kindest & most generous person in the world & few people will ever understand the kindness & hospitality she showed for years to the RAF people stationed in the last war, at Edmonton."

Rina was indeed very ill. Sadly, she died in November 1952. Letters indicate that Ray Milner spent a great deal of time in

Qualicum that winter and in the summer of 1953, perhaps contemplating his future alone and taking solace in the beautiful gardens, ocean and forest Rina had loved. He wrote: "I'm a complete physical and mental wreck. I had no idea before she became ill how deeply attached we were to each other…"

Around the time of his wife's death, Ray purchased the lot from Major Cross. There was a misunderstanding about the trees, a situation that demonstrated both Cross's irrational thinking and Ray's fierce love of the forest. Cross found that Qualicum summers did not agree with him and decided to return to Britain. In September 1952, he wrote to Ray requesting his permission to cut down "half a dozen" trees on the lot in order to protect the powerlines. By November, he wrote to his lawyer claiming Ray had agreed to allow him to log half the lot before the sale was completed! Ray wrote to his lawyer on November 12, 1952: "I would not for a moment think of purchasing Cross's property if there is to be a lumbering operation. The attraction of the place is the virgin forest." And again on December 1: "…so far as I am concerned, any removal of the timber is quite out of the question and no conference in reference to that matter could achieve anything."

After the tree matter was sorted out and the sale completed, Ray had a new, temporary neighbour, Colonel Nigel Bourke. Bourke had a garden in the area, but stayed in Ray's beach cottage for a winter. He was a tall, imposing man and a knowledgeable gardener. He had arrived in Canada as a remittance man and settled in the Okanagan Valley. There, Bourke established an orchard and later, made money by developing land before moving near Qualicum and creating a garden. Colonel Bourke purchased most of his plant material from Ted and Mary Greig's Royston nursery to the

Colonel Bourke.

Ted and Mary Grieg.

north. Bourke was one of their best customers, purchasing many alpines, roses and rhododendrons.

The Greigs were well known in the horticultural community. In 1936, they had bought the nursery stock of Buchanan and Suzanne Simpson. The Greigs were originally interested in alpine plants, especially primulas. When the Simpsons decided to return to Europe, they convinced the Greigs to buy their nursery. Mary wrote:

They rather overpowered us by saying they though (sic) Ted and I should buy it. Apart from being quite astonished to think they thought we could manage to keep things alive, we had practically no money except Ted's salary with the Canadian Colliers and that needed care to keep us afloat.

The Simpsons' nursery and cabin were on a remote shore of Cowichan Lake; several hours' drive south of Royston. "It wasn't possible to walk to them, but if one stood on the Marble Rocks, and shouted someone would eventually hear, and Buchanan rowed over and ferried people across the 100 yards or so to the place," Mary wrote. After some debate, the Greigs bought the nursery stock. Ted drove to Lake Cowichan from Royston every weekend, often with his son Jim. They packed plants into boxes, loaded them on a raft, and rowed across the lake. The plants were then loaded on a home-made trailer, pulled by a Model A Ford truck, and driven to Royston. Every weekend, a few more plants or shrubs were moved. The operation took months.

The Greigs, still interested primarily in alpine plants, dismissed the rhododendrons. According to horticulturalist Allyne Cook, rhododendrons were still fairly exotic and unusual plants for Canadian gardens at the time. Mary wrote: "I remember being quite unimpressed with the species rhododendrons, never having seen any before.... Ted was even less interested so we suggested not bothering bringing those up." Buchanan Simpson assured the Greigs they would soon become fascinated with the plants. Some of these specimens had been obtained from famous plant hunters, including Ludlow and Sherriff, and Frank Kingdon Ward, adventurers who endured hardships in exotic places like China, Borneo, Burma and Japan, sending seeds and plants to England and giving them their Latin names.

The Greigs, especially Mary, did indeed become fascinated and accumulated additional stock by growing seed from England's Sunningdale Nursery, Kew Gardens and the Botanical Gardens at Edinburgh. Their reputation grew to such an extent that, in 1965, they were jointly awarded the American Rhododendron Society Gold Medal.

In March 1953, Ray Milner began to order plants from Ted and Mary Greig's nursery. They had a mutual friend in Bourke, who wrote to Ray about the Greigs. Ray purchased a large order from the Royston nursery, including twenty-four azaleas, four rhododendrons (one R. *chasmanthum*, two *augustinii* and one "Searsiae"), thirty spreading blue perennials (*Gentiana sino-ornata*), and three *Magnolia soulangeana*.

Referring to his friend Colonel Bourke, Ray wrote, "He certainly seems to have a very high regard for you and your husband. I am sure everything will be most satisfactory."

Later that year, again on Colonel Bourke's advice, they discussed planting lilies in front of the house. The Greigs suggested that perhaps Colonel Bourke should supervise the planting rather than trusting the task to the caretaker. On October 26, 1953 the Greigs sent an order of 4 *Lilium humboldti*, 4 *L.* "*Shuksan*," 10 each of *L. regale* and *L. centifolium*, and eight *L.auratum*.

By this time, the orchard of apples, pears and Japanese plums was well established and producing fruit. Bourke suggested a good top dressing of compost. Further, he suggested to Ray that daffodil bulbs should be planted in the orchard meadow grass.

Grass grew on the sea side of the "big" house, but it was not like today's Grand Lawn, as by summer the grass would be parched brown from the sun. In May 1953, Ray wrote to caretaker Robert Strouts:

I have been giving a lot of thought to the lawn between the house and the sea. This year I do not want to tear it up and put on topsoil, but I was quite impressed with a lawn I saw in Vancouver on the way back. The soil, or lack of it, is identical to ours, but with watering and the use of various fertilisers, they have built up a very respectable piece of grass.... Perhaps also we should not use the lawn mower over it this year and give that New Zealand grass a chance to set itself.

By late 1953, the gardens, and Ray, were at a crossroads. With Colonel Bourke's involvement and, more importantly, the introduction of Ray to the Greigs, the garden had become more highly refined. Ray had lost his wife and companion of many years and was close to the apex of his career, an age when many men think of retirement.

CHAPTER SIX

Rays of Light

Our England is a garden, and such gardens are not made
By sighing: — "Oh, how beautiful!" and sitting in the shade,
While better men than we go out and start their working lives
At grubbing weeds from gravel paths with broken dinner-knives.

—Rudyard Kipling

RAY MILNER and a group of Canadian politicians and businessmen met in Ottawa in January 1954 and forged a deal that resulted in the building of the world's largest oil pipeline. The Trans-Canada Pipeline was a remarkable feat, spanning the rugged Canadian North, and was one of the highlights of Ray's career. Perhaps still exhilarated with this recent victory, Ray travelled to England and Ireland later that month to call on Veronica. They attended glamorous parties in London with influential people. The otherwise shrewd businessman was uncharacteristically swept off his feet by Veronica's still stunning beauty. He was smitten. "Moon of my delight," he called Veronica. Friends, relatives and business associates did not understand what had happened to the normally astute Ray, as he suddenly seemed intoxicated with qualities in Veronica that others did not comprehend or appreciate.

On Tuesday, February 2, 1954, Veronica married Ray Milner in St. George's Church, Hanover Square, London. The forty-five-year

Ray and Veronica wed
in London, 1954.

old bride, wearing a crimson satin dress, was given away by her
teenaged son Desmond, now the twenty-ninth Knight of Glin.
The wedding took place under the old church's sixteenth-century
Flemish glass windows, in the fashionable church where Veronica's
mother and father, grandparents and great-grandparents had been
married. The sixty-five-year-old groom wore a top hat and tails.

It is likely that Veronica's motivation for marriage was, at least
in part, financial. Veronica told me that when she married Ray, she
"knew little about him except that he was a conservative." She left
unsaid that he was rich. In some ways, she told me, she never really
knew this quiet, direct man. Ray seemed well aware that money
was a factor in Veronica's decision to marry him. In a letter to her
before their marriage, he asked, "How much do you owe & to
whom?" Ray's wealth seemed to be an issue that was discussed
openly in Veronica's family as well. In 1956, Elaine, Veronica's
mother, wrote that she was pleased that "wonderful Ray (of light)
came along with his *love*, and dollars."

Friends agree the marriage was clearly motivated, in part, by
financial considerations, but all note that Veronica had a clear admiration for Ray. Whereas Desmond had been sickly and perhaps
naive when he married Veronica, Ray was a mature businessman
who had faced many difficulties in life. He likely had a much better
understanding of what he was getting into, and more skills in dealing with her strong personality. Veronica clearly respected Ray in a
way she had not respected Desmond.

In any case, the couple seemed to have had a warm and very af-
fectionate relationship. Ray also seemed to fully enjoy Veronica's
eccentricities. The Dowager Lady Meath remembers Veronica as a
beautiful, talented woman with many admirers. Veronica could be

"quite charming and without complaint." Then, suddenly, she could be "horrible." Ray, she said, was a "delightful man" who knew how to deal with Veronica. She described Ray's reaction to Veronica's sometimes outrageous behaviour. "He would roar with laughter," she said. Veronica's response, in turn, was to "shut up." The union was a remarkable unfolding of the astrologer's predictions for the course of Veronica's life, for 1954 was indeed a "distinctly fortunate" year.

After the wedding, Ray and Veronica travelled to Canada on the *Empress of France*. The ship, refurbished from duties as a troop carrier during the war years, had elegant first-class dining rooms and spacious lounges featuring tasteful carpeting, fine furniture and large windows. By coincidence, Princess Elizabeth and the Duke of Edinburgh had sailed from Liverpool on the ship for a leg of their 1951 tour of Canada in which they stayed at Qualicum. Ray and Veronica landed in Montreal and took the train across Canada, taking until mid-March to reach Qualicum.

Ray's friends and colleagues were exceedingly curious about his mysterious new bride. His friend Colonel Bourke had always been fond of entertaining. He held yearly Christmas parties and, naturally, arranged a cocktail party to greet the new bride and groom. Bourke was a cousin of the Earl of Mayo and related to Veronica's late good friend Lady Eva Bourke, wife of the fifth Earl of Dunraven. He was impressed that Ray had married the widow of the Knight of Glin. Indeed, Bourke and Veronica "spoke the same language," as one of their friends said.

At Bourke's party, Veronica stood in a red silk gown, probably her wedding dress. At six feet, she was several inches taller than Ray. She looked striking; she also looked bored and stiff. She held

Ray, Veronica and Desmond.

Veronica in her red wedding dress.

an unlit cigarette in a long, black holder, obviously waiting for someone to light it. When one brave soul stepped forward to light her cigarette, she inhaled the smoke, but did not acknowledge him. This would herald Veronica's uneasy entry into Qualicum Beach society, a world in which she came to be widely regarded with disfavour. Apparently, Bourke was not surprised. He reportedly said that "everyone" knew that the Guests were the "rudest family in England."

Veronica once again found herself a new bride in a foreign land. This time, however, she was farther from home. In Ireland, she had been able to travel to London fairly often. Here, she felt truly isolated. Qualicum Beach had a population of about 700 at the time. Her maid, Nancy Ellis, recalled how desperately lonely Veronica was in her first year in Canada. She was frequently confined to bed with the "flu" or hives. Veronica even named the estate "Long Distance," "because it was so far away from my old home, and because the telephone was always ringing for my husband."

Nancy was not unsympathetic to Veronica's feelings about Qualicum Beach. There was, she recalled, "no resemblance" between life in Ireland and life in Canada. "I thought it was the end of the world," Nancy said. "Veronica," she recalled, "thought she would die of loneliness." In an early draft of an article on the garden, Veronica's daughter-in-law, Olda FitzGerald, quoted Veronica's characteristically rambling first impressions of her new home in the forest. Veronica recalled lying in bed with the "flu" and gazing out the window:

...*at all those dreary trees and thinking, my God, there's nothing else to do except to plant rhododendrons because nothing else goes with fir trees which I don't like and never have except for the Douglas fir.*

Veronica recalled memories of her grandmother's garden at Canford and its lanes of rhododendrons:

...her 7 mile drive into Bournemouth was lined with these clumps of the strongest growing Ponticum rhododendron, which as well as being very good cover for pheasant shooting somehow looked better than just all those pine trees. Rhododendrons also like acid soil so that's what gave me the idea.

The garden at Canford was typical of gardens popular in Victorian England in which *Rhododendron ponticum* had been grown since the beginning of the nineteenth century. Considered almost a weed in Ireland, they were typically incorporated into "wild garden" areas of estates featuring conifers such as cypress, monkey-puzzle trees and redwoods with an underlay of magnolias.

Rhododendrons planted amid the forest, circa 1965.

Veronica took on the garden at the estate with passion and it became her salvation. Her social class, her artistic talents, her brief education in botany, her exposure to great gardens and garden experts in Ireland, her love of art and flowers and her aristocratic notions of the family estate all led Veronica to take on the challenge of her new home. After receiving a letter describing her garden plans, Elaine responded to her daughter, "I love to think you have gained real happiness after long and difficult years... How thrilling all your garden making sounds. Rhododendrons and pines against the distant sea background sounds too beautiful." Many years later, in a speech at the garden dedication by Malaspina University-

College, Veronica claimed that building the garden was "what any wife" would do for her husband. The crowd chuckled, as the scale of the project was so obviously beyond the reach of "any wife."

Veronica and Mary Greig became friends soon after Veronica's arrival in Canada. Despite class differences, they had a lot in common. Firstly, they shared a love of gardens. Like Veronica, Mary was very familiar with the works of the great Victorian garden writers such as Gertrude Jekyll and Ellen Willmott. Secondly, they were both English. Mary had been born in Bournemouth, very near to Veronica's grandmother's estate at Canford. Mary was impressed with Veronica's connection to Churchill and the British aristocracy. Like Veronica, Mary had little formal education, having quit school at age fourteen. Mary's son Jim described his mother as an extremely intelligent woman who needed "someone like Veronica" for mental stimulation.

Veronica needed strong, direct, no-nonsense people around her. It helped if they had a sense of humour. Ray was like that, and so was Mary. Mary was the kind of woman who "didn't suffer fools gladly." Alleyne Cook recalled, "In our house, she was always known as Mrs. No-Nonsense Greig. Once when the entire family was departing after a happy weekend she said, 'I'm glad you came, I enjoyed you being here, I'm pleased you are all leaving.'" Mary's son Jim and his wife recall that, when shoppers would stop by the Royston nursery wanting annuals, Mary would say, "We don't sell tomato plants. We don't sell annuals. Goodbye," shutting the door on shocked faces.

Ray and Ted were also very fond of one another. Like Ray, Ted Greig had served overseas during the Great War. Ted was a physically strong man, known to hike up a mountain carrying a 120-

Mary Grieg.

pound pack on his back. When purchases were made from the nursery, he would deliver them to the garden in his homemade trailer and often plant them himself, an insurance that they were properly taken care of. His old truck made frequent trips from Royston to Qualicum. Throughout the 1950s and 60s, the Greigs were often guests at Qualicum.

With the collaboration of Ted and Mary Greig, Veronica began to plan the expansion of the garden. In the first years that she was mistress of "Long Distance," hundreds of rhododendrons were planted, many beneath and amid the forest trees. Within a short time, most of the existing rhododendrons were in place. Magnolias and Chinese dogwood were purchased from Hyland Barnes' Vancouver nursery in about 1954. The sensuous, profusely blooming, tropical-looking magnolias had great appeal for Veronica. The tree remains stately all year round. In spring, it produces soft-petalled, loosely cupped, exotic-looking flowers in blush pinks or whites. The delicate star magnolia (*Magnolia stellata*) is planted in an area sheltered from the wind, but close enough to the house for the occupants to enjoy the spring display.

Several purchases are documented in correspondence with the Greigs, the primary source of plant material. On September 12, 1964, Mary wrote to Ray and Veronica listing the totals of plants bought from the Royston nursery in the years 1953 to 1964. The total came to $4,835.74. Mary wrote:

> *Here is your list, Ray. I knew you had been marvellous customers but neither of us realised how marvellous. About $1000 of it did not come from this garden, particularly the large azaleas, but very nice business anyway. Thank you! Thank goodness we have never charged for time or we should feel like Robin Hood.*

Magnolia x soulangeana.

This last comment was no doubt in reference to certain resentment or dissimilarity that Mary Greig, who struggled financially, was always conscious of, in dealing with the relatively wealthy Milners. Despite their common interests and friendly relationship, class differences were still acute in Canada. While Veronica extolled her aristocratic roots to all who would listen, Ted worked as a shipping clerk and then paymaster at Canadian Colliers at Union Bay, north of Qualicum Beach. He retired without a pension at age fifty-eight. Mary, meanwhile, ran the nursery and cared for the

children. Over time, Ted came to dislike Veronica for her snobbery and would snort at the mention of her name. However, both Ray and Veronica appreciated the Greigs' contribution to the garden. At one point, the Milners paid for a vacation for the Greigs to the Hawaiian island of Maui. Mary was uneasy accepting such generosity. The Greigs repaid their hosts by surprising them with a bed of deciduous azaleas that still stands, a blaze of gold and orange glory in the spring, across from the master bedroom.

Eventually, the Greigs decided to name one of their rhododendrons, which still exists in the Milners' garden, in honour of Veronica. On April 13, 1957, Mary wrote to Veronica:

We've got one really lovely little hybrid of our own in flower — R. campylocarpu x Little Ben, which is a clear brilliant pink. We sort of dally now with a name — would you like to choose it? Mrs. R.H. Milner — Veronica — Long Distance — what do you think? We shall have to propagate it now, and you shall have the first fruits. Think about it and tell us when we see you next.

A September 1964 letter to the Milners from Mary suggests she was plotting the garden and working on the large plantings of camellias, trees and vines close to the house. Mary's rough list records the purchase of:

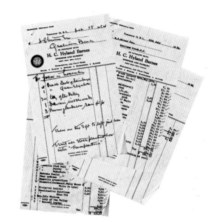

Three *Acer palmatum*
one *Acer schwedleri* 'Nigra'
Betula riversii
Camelia Pink Bell
Camellia Purity
Camellia Wakankura
three *Cornus florida* 'Rubra'
3 *Cornus florida* 'Alba'
Cherry- P. Yae Kwazan
Daphne Somerset
Magnolia kobus borealis
Magnolia parviflora

soulangeana nigra
soulangeana pink
stellata
Pieris japonica 3
Viburun carlesii 3
Viburum carlcephalum 1
Wisteria, shrubby, purple 2
Wisteria, shrubby, pink 1
Clematis Jackmanii
Clematis Nellie Moser
Clematis Ville de Lyon

A list in Mary's handwriting is named "Copy of plants sold April 29, 1965." It includes the following:

1 R. Brocade   4 (rock)
2 *pemakocuse* @ $5   10
2 Sapphire @ $5   10

1	Mary Greig	10 (steps)
1	*degronianium*	3.50
1	large Rose *calostrotum*	6.00
1	*chapmanii*	4.00
1	spinuliferam hybrid	5.00 (Blue Bell)
1	myiagrum	8.00 T. Court
1	Royal Lady	4.00 T. Court
1	Carmen x F.C. Puddle	5.00
1	charlopes	4.50
1	*hypophaeordes* Haba Shar	3.50
1	*psendoyaulthum*	4.50
3	*cosmetum*	7.50 Rockery
1	*nussalum*	5.00
1	*impedetum*	3.50
		98.00
	Tax	4.90
		102.90

Mary wrote a short letter to Veronica describing yet another shipment of plants for the garden. Mary wrote: "Perhaps it might be wise to leave the sino-grande in the greenhouse here until next spring. The older they are the better their chance of survival, I think. That one is only 5 or six years old. The sizes I've given are present ones, not eventual, of course. Much love, Mary."

According to Veronica, one of the first tasks in the Qualicum garden had been to correct the water situation that had plagued it for years. Veronica declared that she was a dowser, able to detect the presence of water underground using only a forked twig. As her eccentric artist friend Gibbings had instructed her in Ireland,

Top left: The house, circa 1965; top right: Azaleas – a gift from the Greigs; above: Camelias.

she grasped the twig, one fork in each hand. Muscles twitched. The twig bent toward the earth. Sure enough, she found water and a well was built.

Around the same time, Ted Greig was developing a plan to redirect and reroute the existing open drainage to form a small stream. Ray was delighted with Ted's ideas and wrote to Nigel Bourke: "Quite obviously our friend Greig has given a lot of thought to the matter and has produced a very ingenious suggestion. Whether I could undertake the job without the certainty of going broke is, however, another question." The Milners went ahead with the work, hiring a local contractor to complete the rockwork around the ponds and making other improvements. Una Bourke, Veronica's maid and confidante, also came to live at Qualicum. On April 24, 1956, she wrote to Veronica:

The garden is looking lovely and all the shrubs are doing well, the Azaleas are beginning to flower, and the rhododendrons also, and the prunus trees in front of your bedroom are in blossom. I do hope they will hold until you come

Chinese Dogwood

back, the Roses in the Rose-bed are just beginning to leaf. The men have been cementing inside the little pond on the Rockery, but so far haven't done anything to the patio, but I expect they will be.

Another early task was to open up the forest in order to form the glades. These were clearly built in a fashion that allowed views from the veranda. The stand of trees near the meadow includes the dove or handkerchief tree (*Davidia involucrata*), whose bracts shimmer in the spring sun, the Japanese maple (*Acer palmatum*) that turns crimson in the fall, and the Chinese dogwood (*Cornus kousa* var. *chinensis*), creamy white in June. These were planted to be viewed from a distance. The tall European white birch (*Betula pendula*) is like a swath of paint on a forest canvas. It is a mark of genius, a fountain of light against the dark forest. Frames in the trees were cut or pruned to expose a perfect view. Veronica also wanted the garden to be a "welcome habitat for wildlife, particularly birds. We had to open up glades to let in the light and drain excess water into pools for the birds to drink in."

It is clear from the existing letters that Ray, like Veronica's first husband, had always taken an active interest in the garden. It is likely that he continued to do so after his marriage to Veronica. He was not just a passive person holding an open chequebook, although he was certainly generous to his new wife. Indeed, Ray was a thoughtful man and would likely have restrained Veronica's impulsive tendencies. It is easy to imagine Veronica and Mary, and probably Ray and Ted, walking through the glades, pen and pencil in hand, making notes and suggestions, driving stakes in the ground to place large specimens. And after, perhaps having tea on the veranda.

One of Ray's interests continued to be in protecting the forest. As the rhododendron grove grew to extensive dimensions under forest trees, Ted tried to convince Ray to cut down trees to give the rhododendrons more light. Ray refused. This presented a situation that would not be rectified for many years until an arborist, contracted by Malaspina University-College, also protested that the rhododendrons were suffering, and some threatened, by the insufficient light in the forest.

When Veronica came to the garden, it contained second growth and remnants of old-growth forest. There were some existing trees, such as the chestnut, hawthorn, and the newly planted rhododendrons. In her first years at Qualicum, Veronica transformed these beginnings into a Canadian adaptation of the English woodland garden nestled in the trees, a "wild garden." The house, woods, orchard and rhododendron grove and lawn were built in harmony with one another and with nature. In summer, there were no mass displays of "vulgar" bedding plants planted in what William Robinson would have called "garden graveyards." There were none of the "evil practices" of many sterile gardens. This would be a place of serenity, elegance, rhythm and harmony. "In tune with the Infinite," as Veronica would have said.

Veronica described the planning of the garden by the "topography of the land" and the "salubrious" climate of the Qualicum area. The garden had no master plan. "I did it on my own," Veronica claimed. She chose trees and imagined them at full growth, thirty or forty feet, confident in Mary's horticultural expertise, especially as it relates to the rhododendrons. Letters from Mary often gave specific directions for plantings. Veronica was the artist with the vision. She had the iron will, and money, to make the

Acer palmatum and Betula pendula.

vision happen. Veronica never claimed to be a plant or garden expert, and credited Mary with the technical knowledge. Hired help performed most of the manual tasks. This is entirely in keeping with Veronica's world view. It was how she described the functioning of her beloved British Empire. According to this view, the aristocracy had the vision and drive; the professional classes provided the specific knowledge to implement the vision and the lower classes provided the brawn to carry out the task. George Abbey had also expressed this idea. In a 1909 edition of the *Journal of Horticulture*, Abbey acknowledged the role of the artist in the development of the "wild garden," that is woodlands embellished with exotics and native wild flowers and carried out by hired help. Abbey wrote: "Such gardens – that is to say, the present time wild garden, for instance – do not require to be made by gardeners; any person possessing a painter's eye, and assisted by country labourers…will form them just as well as a landscape gardener."

Clearly the philosophy and tastes of William Robinson, as taught by Sir Frederick Moore, and demonstrated in gardens like her grandmother's, and especially at Mount Usher in Ireland, had an enormous influence on Veronica, and, therefore, on the garden. "This is a garden, not a park," Veronica often told us in reference to the kind of chaos she preferred. This was not to be a garden of carefully mowed, weedless lawns. Buttercups bob in the grass. Masses of forget-me-nots shine periwinkle blue. Weeds, birds and specimen trees live in symphony. The garden paid tribute to native plant materials at a time when bedding plants and slick, sculptured lawns were prevalent in North American gardens. Again, Robinson explicitly expressed strong views about such matters:

Surely it is enough to have a portion of lawn as smooth as a carpet at all

Photo of Veronica,
dated October, 1956.

times, without shaving off the 'long and pleasant grass' of other parts of the grounds... Mowing the grass once a fortnight in pleasure grounds, as now practiced, is a costly mistake. *He goes on to say: "*Not *to mow is almost a necessity in the wild garden. . ."* [emphasis his]

Above and below: Mt. Usher. Both the gardens at Mount Usher and at Qualicum feature *Metasequoia glyptostroboides* (dawn redwood).

Photographs of Mount Usher show marked similarities with the Milners' garden. Most of the plants Robinson recommended are growing at the garden, and are laid out in similar fashion.

Veronica spoke about the garden with the language of an artist. She used her artistic eye in designing the garden and likely relied heavily on her early training in art employing the principles of painting and composition. She was concerned with shape, texture, colours, tone and, above all, the harmony of the whole garden. Veronica believed that gardening was the highest form of art, another view shared by Robinson and the Victorians. Robinson wrote: "True gardening differing from all other arts in this that it gives the living things themselves, and not merely representations of them in paint or stone or wood." This was not a new idea, however. Horace Walpole (1717–97) was one of the first to theorize that a garden should be understood as an art. Poetry, painting and gardening were the "Three Sisters" who "dress and adorn nature."

As well as all she had obviously absorbed from Moore and Robinson, much of Veronica's knowledge was likely derived from her quite incredible powers of observation. She did not have a formal education in horticulture, or landscape architecture, and only the briefest formal education in botany, yet she had a tremendous understanding of the environment. She could spend hours watching and listening. Veronica travelled a great deal and would have seen many trees in their mature size, perhaps in their native habitat. A

Bark of Acer Griseum.

tree might be chosen for the beauty of branches in the winter, and its contrast to, and complement with, the forest. She was able to anticipate form and texture and colour, as she waited to see the fruits of her planning.

There are plants that did not thrive. Perhaps they were planted in the wrong place, or were too fragile for the climate. Perhaps colours clashed, the soil was too impoverished, or the plant too vigorous. For some, the ocean blew too hard or the air was too damp. Some were planted too close to others. Veronica was a plantswoman who collected plants for their own sake and put them in the ground, at times, in hodgepodge fashion, leaving some areas less attractive than others. She was not deterred by errors. Tom Wall, gardener at Glin for almost thirty years, recalled that Veronica "had the feel of the place and no one could distract her. No one else had a say that a plant or tree was in the wrong place. If they proved to be planted too close, she would not move them. 'They can go away together,' she would say."

When I met her, Veronica had only the vaguest memories of the origins of many plants and trees. She was not primarily concerned with what this plant or that was called. This is an idea once again compatible with Robinson's view that "to concern oneself entirely with nomenclature and classification, is not the gardening spirit, it is the *life* we want." Tom Wall recalled, however, that when she was younger she had a tremendous memory for the names of plants and their origins, and recalled, "She knew precisely what she wanted, and was always visualizing down the line. She had a fantastic memory for how things were doing, how she came to get a certain plant, she knew the precise botanical names of every plant in the garden." He noted, however, that her botanical interests were

Hydrangeas.

limited. She was only interested in certain plants, usually different forms of the same genus of plants.

Veronica told stories of collecting seeds and cuttings on her travels. She was inspired, for example, by visits to Corfu, where, she said, "all things lovely for the garden" originated. Whether the stories about the origins of some plants are factual is difficult to determine. Some are documented. Her papers contain letters dated 1963 from the Canada Department of Agriculture authorizing the importation of several plants including *Jasminum gracillinum, Juniperus chinensis, Osmanthus fragrans* and *Jasminum sambac* from Kawahara Nursery and Landscaping Company in Honolulu. An Edmonton friend wrote to tell Veronica her mother had some specimens for her: "Perhaps you should take possession of them while you are in England and slip them in your pocket for the journey." This collection was to include "Littleworth Cross Rhododendron, *falconeri-nightii, hodgsonii* and *griffinthianum x decorum*." Veronica claimed her *Platanus occidentalis* seed came directly from the original tree that Hippocrates sat under on the Island of Cos. The original tree, forty-six feet in circumference in 1966, is estimated to be over 2,500 years old.

Veronica declared that she collected the seed for a spectacular Japanese maple on a trip to Japan in 1968. The *Euonymus alatus* (winged spindle tree or burning bush), she recalled, was a gift from Colonel Bourke. She told the story of another of the trees: "Ray and I were driving up from Victoria and saw a small pot at the side of the road, at a house, not even a nursery. They were trying to sell it." The Milners stopped and bought the maple sapling, now a majestic tree.

Veronica imported hydrangeas from Glin, from the plants originally given to Desmond and her by Lord Dunraven early in their marriage. She brought fuchsias and camellias, originally from Tarbert House in County Kerry. On each visit to Glin, Veronica would pack moist cuttings in plastic bags into suitcases and eventually plant them at Qualicum, with varying results. For example, Tom reported that the fuchsias, used as hedging mate-

Fushia growing at Glin.

rials around Irish fields, seem to thrive in Atlantic ocean winds so that they need drastic pruning every November. At Qualicum, fuchsias grow well, but are much less vigorous.

The myrtle at Glin, like the fuchsia and camellias, are from County Kerry and a garden created by the Knights of Kerry, kinsmen of the Knights of Glin. In Ireland, the freely seeding plants grow "like an epidemic," in Tom's words. They were, however, difficult to establish at Qualicum. Veronica repeatedly took cuttings of myrtle, perhaps thirty at a time, in her suitcase. "She kept digging up more to take to Canada," Tom recalled. Finally, she had success, and myrtle now grows outside the door to the house. Veronica also took young beech trees, perhaps two or three inches high, and eucryphia, for the garden at Qualicum. Conversely, she would bring plant material from Canada to Glin. Most notable in this effort were rhododendrons. Veronica would complain that the only rhododendrons available in Ireland were those grafted onto ponticum, which soon reverted.

As a result of the transportation of so much plant material

between Glin and Qualicum, there are striking similarities and contrasts between the two gardens. While Glin sits near the outstretched mouth of the Shannon, Qualicum is on protected ocean. Winds blow heavily off the Atlantic in winter, while Qualicum is fairly shielded. Glin has four inches of clay-type topsoil and poor subsoil, while Qualicum has a sandy, acidic soil. Both locations enjoy moderate temperatures, although there is much more rain at Glin, especially in the summer months. While water has always been an issue at Qualicum, irrigation at Glin is not required.

The similarities with Qualicum are most in evidence in the informal parts of the garden at Glin. Spanish chestnuts in both gardens recall the gardens at Canford. Each contains magnolias, rhododendrons, wisteria, bluebells and roses. Glin has an avenue

"Wild garden" at Glin.

of palm trees. Although palm trees would likely be hardy to Qualicum, none are in the garden.

Glin was established at an earlier time and social factors contributed to its design. The gardens near the castle were laid out by Veronica and are influenced by European formal gardens. These are suited to the implied status that a "castle" and title represent. The gardens at Qualicum, on the other hand, developed purely for the pleasure of friends and family, were relatively casual in nature. The "wild garden" concept at Qualicum may have been especially attractive as the house was primarily meant as a summer home and this type of garden is relatively low maintenance.

Over Veronica's early years in Qualicum, the house evolved as well as the garden. The original gardener lived in a room attached to the garage until a small gardener's cottage was built. In the early 1960s, Veronica arranged for the tiny cottage to be expanded. As the Milners spent more time at Qualicum, suitable extensions and additions grew. The original wooden steps at the front of the house were replaced, and the drawing room windows lowered. The pool (originally filled with saltwater pumped from the ocean below) and tennis courts were built before 1964. Many of the new garden purchases were related to these various improvements. A fully automatic underground sprinkler system was installed in August 1967.

Builder Don Beaton first drew up plans for a proposed addition to the house in the fall of 1957. He then wrote that the plan "...has progressed beyond our first discussions in both size and cost. It would definitely be attractive in appearance and more easily managed than a separate unit." The addition, known as the

The new "studio" circa 1968.

"studio," would contain a "main room," study, kitchen, powder room, storage closet and bar. That fall, Ray sent a telegram telling Don Beaton to go ahead and begin the project. It was apparently not completed, however. Around the same time, Veronica's son Desmond moved to Vancouver to study at the University of British Columbia. He graduated with a B.A. in 1959 and then went to Harvard University for his M.A. in Fine Arts.

Arthur Erickson, the famous Canadian architect, was a friend of Desmond from his undergraduate days in Vancouver. Erickson had designed a house in Comox, some forty miles to the north of Qualicum, and would often stop to visit. Veronica wanted to expand the house and continually imposed upon him to draw up plans. When he finally did produce a proposal, dated June 2, 1959, it failed to live up to Veronica's expectations. She was scornful and felt Erickson's ideas were not consistent with the "cottage" character of the house. Instead, Veronica and Don Beaton revised the plans once again. According to Veronica, the idea for an unusual angular fireplace that allows a view to the ocean was her own. It is not clear when the studio was finally completed, but a note in the family guest book dated July 1968 reads: "here's to the new studio." It is worth noting that the couple that wrote the comment had last visited in the summer of 1967. In any event, once completed, the studio was used to entertain, perhaps for bridge and dinner. Guests stayed there, and later, Veronica used it as a painting studio. Ray used one room as his private study.

In addition to the work under taken at Qualicum, Ray and Veronica often travelled to Ireland and continued to be involved with the castle at Glin. Ray paid for an extensive renovation to Glin. As noted, Paddy Healy had been a good friend to Desmond and the Healy family had been connected with the castle for generations. Veronica had great respect for Paddy and persuaded him to take on the massive task of renovations. "We never had a word," she would say about him, a high compliment indeed. Many letters travelled to and fro between Canada and Ireland as the house was rewired and all the battlements removed and reinstated. The forty ton slate roof was replaced with two tons of Canadian shingles, a project that Ray was especially interested in. Much else was done at a time in Ireland when there was very little employment.

Ray was also involved in the purchase of cattle for the castle farm. Veronica, at her son Desmond's urging, was involved in supporting a gift shop, an enterprise set up to help support the castle. The Castle Gate shop sold fresh bread, soup, scones and ice cream. It also sold rush baskets, tweed, scarves, shawls, mohair caps and stoles and necklaces from Connemara. Although forced to commercialize, the shop only featured the "best quality Irish goods available." Desmond wrote to his mother, "There are a lot of these and we do not need to lower our sights into vulgar plastic gnomes, shamrock paperweights, leprechauns, shileighs, etc!!"

Ray became increasingly concerned about Veronica's extravagant tastes and the cost of renovating both Glin and the various garden and building projects at Qualicum. In 1960, Veronica took an extended trip to Portugal and England to visit her daughter Fiola. Ray wrote to her:

Do be as careful of expenditures as you reasonably can. I'm afraid of the old well drying up before we have finished drinking. Our expenses are tremendous.

A few days later, he put things in more blunt terms: "No money is to be spent on Glin this summer…" Over time, however, the renovations at Glin were complete and the farm established. The castle was rented out to various parties during the 1960s and 1970s. Eventually, Veronica's son Desmond, now married and starting a family, moved permanently to Glin. By the mid-1980s, it was open to the public as a hotel, offering fine dining and a unique historic setting. The unfinished top floor was completed in 1999 with five additional bedrooms and bathrooms. Glin became increasingly attractive as an exclusive stopping place for golfers and tourists.

At Qualicum during this time, gardeners came and went. The Strouts had long ago tired of Veronica's imperious ways and moved on. A gardener named Laurie Halliday especially impressed Ray Milner. In March 1961, Halliday left the garden to work on a Rockland Avenue estate in Victoria. Ray wrote a short note: "I am very sorry you are leaving us the end of this month. Under your supervision the grounds and gardens have been improved tremendously. You certainly have been diligent and hard working." Ray rewarded this diligence and hard work with a $100 bonus. Don Beaton's company did much of the major clearing or digging requiring machinery. A November 1965 invoice indicates Qualicum Construction was involved in tasks ranging from clearing a plugged toilet to installing gate posts and split cedar fence posts.

Veronica tended to spend more time at Qualicum than Ray, who was still involved with business dealings. Nancy and Una, the maids who had moved with her from Ireland, stayed at Qualicum all the time. Veronica's personal account books for several years detailed their combined salary of $120 per month. Nancy vividly recalled working long hours cooking, cleaning and tending to Veronica's personal needs. Late at night, she and Una climbed the steep stairs to the small attic room they shared under the rafters. Even this was not always enough. Nancy recalled being woken in the night by Veronica with the directive to "go downstairs and take four salmon out of the freezer. There will be twenty guests for dinner."

Ray and Veronica also had an apartment in Edmonton and Ray had offices in both Calgary and Edmonton. He owned the "Old Hermitage" farm near Edmonton and raised award-winning Aberdeen Angus bulls. Alberta winters are dry and cold while summertime often brings severe thunderstorms; Veronica would not have enjoyed these extremes. When I asked Veronica about Edmonton, she would only roll her eyes and seemed to have little affection for the city.

Veronica joined several garden-related organizations. In May 1967, she was asked to stand for election to the Board of Governors of the Vancouver Botanical Gardens Association. According to sev-

Helleborus orientalis.

eral sources, however, she was fairly inactive in this role. Yet the June 13, 1973 minutes of the board meeting note that Veronica was accepted as an honorary member of the Board of Governors. With contributions from the Vancouver Foundation, and funds from the Province and the City of Vancouver, the organization evolved into the VanDusen Botanical Gardens. Although her role may have been small, it introduced to her people such as botanical illustrator Mary Comber-Miles and her husband Victor, who would eventually become very good friends.

A long-time member of the International Dendrology Society, Veronica also became a fellow of the Garden Conservancy, a member of the Royal Horticultural Society and a member of the Royal Society of Arts and Commerce. As well, Veronica joined the Devonian Botanical Garden at the University of Alberta. She continued many of these associations throughout her life. Her private sitting room contained a library of garden reference books and journals. She would attend lectures and several important rhododendron specialists came to Vancouver Island at the invitation of the well-respected Greigs. Like the Greigs, she was a member of the Vancouver chapter of the American Rhododendron Society.

The Milners' garden began to come to international attention. In July 1970, the Horticultural Society of New York visited the garden on a tour of the Pacific Northwest and Alaska. Organizer Edith Crockett wrote, "I certainly would not wish our group to miss seeing your place, as it is certainly one of the most fascinating that I have seen."

While the garden flourished, Ray continued his lifetime interest in politics. On December 14, 1956, John Diefenbaker was elected leader of the federal Progressive Conservative Party. Veronica and

Ray attended the convention. According to Veronica, Ray was distressed at the election of Diefenbaker. Ray reportedly declared uncharacteristically, "That man is not fit to be a lawyer, never mind Prime Minister." Veronica, too, was more than unimpressed. She was with a group of Conservative women when Diefenbaker's wife, Olive, approached wearing what Veronica described as a "hideous" hat covered with ribbons. "How dare that woman even *speak* to *me*?" Veronica asked. This was an event that seemed to hold special significance for Veronica as she told me the story again and again, the anger and affront still palpable after over forty years.

Veronica invariably accompanied Ray on his many world-wide jaunts. Never involved in his business affairs, she would shop or see the sights while he attended meetings. The house and gardens at the Milner Estate reflect their travels, taste and interests. Wallpaper outside the dining room has a Chinese motif, and was purchased on a vacation to Paris. Ornamental sculptures add accent and interest to the garden. These were often purchased during travels, gifts from Ray to Veronica. A lead sundial in the form of a kneeling slave is an example of such a gift. It was typical of the classical themes that reflected good taste in the eighteenth century English garden. Another of the classical group is the Boy on a Dolphin, set close to the woodland stream amid maid-

Oriental screen purchased on a trip to Japan in 1968.

127

Kneeling slave sundial – 1998 (top & above) and 1968 (lower right).

enhair fern, hostas, azaleas, day lilies and irises. The statue was purchased near Boston when Veronica's son Desmond graduated with a Master's degree from Harvard University. Ray bought two bronze Chinese cranes in New York on a trip during the winter of 1964–65. (Veronica told us that when the birds were first installed in the garden, a live heron was observed making amorous gestures toward a potential metallic mate.) In 1968, Ray and Veronica travelled to Japan for the launching of the SS *Golar Ron* for Ocean Oil Enterprises. A lovely oriental screen that decorated Ray's Qualicum office was purchased on the trip.

Ray was an avid connoisseur of fine art and collected silver, bronze and art, particularly Canadian paintings. He owned several paintings by the Montreal-born painter James Wilson Morrice, a Paris-based artist who earned an international reputation. Ray had a large collection of paintings by Group of Seven artists Arthur Lismer, Frederick Varley, Frank Carmichael, A.Y. Jackson and Lawren Harris, as well as two works by Emily Carr. He had a fine collection of Remington bronzes, a Henry Moore sculpture (*Reclining Woman*), an early Ming Dynasty water vessel, and a sixteenth Century Buddha, to name a few.

Ray and Veronica also began to meet artists in Canada. The English portrait painter Bernard Hailstone was commissioned by

Ray's company to paint his portrait in 1967. Hailstone had painted portraits of Winston Churchill and Earl Mountbatten before his arrival in Canada. He painted Ray's portrait while a guest at Qualicum. The Milners met Victoria artist Edward (Teddy) Goodall and his wife Carol in the early 1970s. The Goodalls frequently spent several days as guests while Teddy painted in the garden. Many of his lovely watercolours, with views of the house and garden, remain in the house.

Veronica studied at the Banff School of Fine Arts near Calgary. She had, in addition, other more surprising pastimes. One evening, when we came to visit, we found Veronica engrossed in a televised football game, in which she showed clearly more than a passing interest. When I asked her where her interest in football came from, she explained that Ray and some business associates had a box at the stadium in Edmonton. They attended many, many Edmonton Eskimo matches. Ray and his associates watched the game, while Veronica knitted contentedly.

Through the 1950s and 1960s, Ray began to be rewarded with honours for his lifetime of work. Dalhousie University gave him an honorary doctorate in May 1954. He was also awarded honorary doctorates from Mount Allison University, King's University and the University of Alberta. The Salvation Army awarded him the army's Order of Distinguished Auxiliary Service in 1957. On May 4, 1958, Ray was installed as chancellor of the University of King's College. In 1959, an office tower was opened in Edmonton, named for Ray.

On April 8, 1970, Ray was invested as a Companion of the Order of Canada at Government House in Ottawa. The award, established by Prime Minister Lester Pearson in 1967, is the high-

Ray Milner.

est honour Canada gives to her outstanding and distinguished citizens. Governor General Roland Michener presented the award to the recipients, including Ray's friend and fellow Albertan, Ernest Manning. That year, only nine Canadians were invested as Companions of the Order, while an additional nineteen were recipients of the medal of service.

The Milners entertained family, business associates, visitors from the United States, Britain and local friends at the Qualicum estate. Ray's business partner George Steer, and his wife Skippy were frequent guests, as was George Walker and his wife Gladys. Walker was chairman of CPR and Ray described him as "one of my oldest and closest friends." Ray's secretary, Miss Chisholm, typically spent a week in summer at Qualicum. Veronica's son Desmond, his wife and children also came to visit each summer. The children swam in the pool or at the beach. One of Olda's letters describes a family visit in the summer of 1974:

The pool.

It was a dream come true — day after day of that glorious weather and you and Ray to talk to and boost us up and give us encouragement and good advise — and all that marvellous food and attention...oh for lunch at the pool! And that scrumptious sweet corn — the whole thing was so heavenly....

Vegetables for the table were grown in the kitchen garden using organic methods. Veronica's tastes tended to be very English. She was fond of neither salad greens nor tomatoes, but she liked carrot and turnip mashed together, beans, beets and peas. She loved asparagus as a special treat served with lemon and melted butter, a separate course eaten with fingers. Fresh berries from the berry garden were made into preserves.

Dinner was an elaborate social ritual reminiscent of an earlier time. Guests were never to assist in service. "Don't help the help!" Veronica would declare. "Only Americans do that!" Wine and conversation accompanied each course. After dinner, Veronica rose from the table and led the women to the drawing room, while the men remained to smoke cigars and drink port. In the tradition of British regiments, the port was always passed in a decanter to the person on the left, never crossing the table. Formal dinners were in the dining room, more informal family affairs might include a picnic on the beach, or later, by the pool. Despite her general efforts to please, carried out in directives to staff, Veronica could be rude to guests she did not like, friends recall. Ray would put Veronica in her place: "Don't talk such nonsense."

Over time, Nancy recalled, the Milners did less and less entertaining. Ray officially retired from the utilities companies in 1962, but continued as a member of several boards of directors and maintained offices in Alberta. He finally retired in 1969 at age eighty and spent many of his remaining days at Qualicum. Ray died at home in Qualicum on Saturday, May 24, 1975 at age eighty-six. He was buried in Edmonton near Rina.

Dining room.

CHAPTER SEVEN

Alone Again

I hold it as a changeless law,
From which no soul can sway or swerve,
We have that in us which will draw
Whate'er we need or most deserve.

— Ralph Waldo Trine

ACCORDING TO Veronica's friend Mary Hughes, Veronica changed when Ray died. "The person who had always listened to her, her anchor, was gone." Ray had protected and understood her for over twenty years. He also had been able to generate the funds to support Veronica's relatively elaborate lifestyle. On her own, she was acutely aware of being despised by many. She told a friend, "You can't think how appalling it is to walk into a room and know everyone dislikes you." Veronica often told me she felt misunderstood. She could not talk to Canadians, she said, because "people in Canada do not speak the same language." One of her early friends noted that the hostility Veronica experienced was because "people didn't understand where she came from, her different life." This certainly may be part of the explanation, but it is far from the whole story. Her behaviour and sense of her own importance offended many people. Veronica's unpleasant conduct seems

Veronica's paintings.

to have increased after Ray's death, perhaps exacerbated by an increasing desperation to maintain her lifestyle and preserve her garden. A letter written by her brother Amherst in 1979, after one of their many spats, expresses what many felt:

Ray would never have behaved like that — wonderful generous man that he always was — but the fact is dear Veronica if people don't fit into your latest plan & picture you drop them like a hot cake — I'd rather have my hair too long and wear the wrong clothes than earn that reputation.

Veronica could also be jealous and possessive. One of her long-time friends was Mary Hughes, a delightful woman who would invite Veronica to lunch and to sketch in her lovely Port Alberni garden. Mary, a talented artist, was invited to join the Federation of Canadian Artists when her name had been put forward after a gallery exhibition of her paintings. It was not an association Mary sought, but she gracefully accepted the honour. When Veronica heard about it, she was enraged. The matter was made worse when Veronica submitted photographs of her own paintings, only to have them rejected.

Veronica could be disagreeable for no apparent purpose. I witnessed a situation when house guests were not allowed to use the telephone or the swimming pool after long hours of travel on a hot summer day. She was extremely outspoken and would voice her opinions in no uncertain terms, with no apparent empathy for the subject of her wrath. At times, she would bang her fist on the table and say, *"I have spoken!!"* in the most imperious manner, clearly enjoying the sound of her own words.

Over the years, an increasing number of people distanced themselves from Veronica. She would play bridge with a group of

Veronica and Mary
Greig in garden
(circa 1976–77).

women friends. For many years, Mary Greig played in this group.
Ted Greig passed away in 1967, so Veronica would send one of her
staff up to Royston in the car to pick Mary up. Mary would often
bring a rhododendron as a gift for her hostess. Over time, even
Mary wanted less to do with her friend. Veronica's rude behaviour
created a tension that spoiled the evening and Mary began to find
reasons not to visit.

Yet, Veronica described the period after Ray's death as her "heyday." She was a widow again, but this time she was in a far better
financial position than she had been when widowed in Ireland.
Her children were grown and less of a concern. She spent many
hours painting with friends in her garden and studio, producing
several large still lifes and flower pieces that adorned the house.
She continued to travel: Mexico, Europe, Hawaii, Australia, Ireland and the Mediterranean. She visited the Channel Islands and
toured logging operations in Sweden and Norway. She travelled to
Australia with the Dendrology Society. Several of her friends re-

member Veronica travelling with an impossibly large number of cumbersome suitcases — more than could fit into the car, or cabin or hotel room, never having learned the art and value of packing light. She kept leather suitcases, her name printed on them in gold. At the airport, there were inevitably difficulties with her baggage, with airline employees "typing on the computer waiting to see if others did not fly with a full load of baggage," gardener Tom Wall recalled.

In January 1981, Veronica left for a three-week West Indies Garden Tour sponsored by the Centre for Continuing Education at the University of British Columbia. The twenty-two garden enthusiasts, under the guidance of David Tarrant, then education coordinator of the UBC Botanical Garden, visited brilliant gardens and plantations in the Dominican Republic and Barbados. They visited a spice farm on Grenada, tropical jungles and giant fern trees, private and botanical gardens. Veronica in turn amused and annoyed other participants on the tour by pointing her long finger and insisting her bags be taken care of, as if they were only along to ensure her comfort and pleasure.

For several years, Veronica employed servants from India. During their stay, the house ran with smooth perfection. Many friends described this time as a pleasant period. The staff was friendly and efficient. One friend remembered arriving at the house on a rainy day, only to be met by a servant in a white jacket, holding an umbrella over her head to protect her from the rain. In those days, Veronica drove the car. She would come upon closed gates on the drive and honk ceaselessly on the horn until one of the servants came to open the gates.

Veronica continued to befriend like-minded residents of Qual-

Veronica and her staff prepare for the Queen's visit. Back row: "Raju" Amirtharaju, Arul Amirtharaju, "Pat" Chuallah. Front row: Veronica and Beth Johnston (secretary).

icum. One of these was Commander Clive Gwinner. As a convoy escort group commander, Gwinner had been a wartime hero who played an immense role in the Battle of the Atlantic. In June 1944, his submarines had ensured that the D-Day armada was shielded from German U-boats. After the war, he was posted to command in Hong Kong and then Burma. Gwinner retired to Qualicum in 1978. He was described in his lengthy 1998 *Daily Telegraph* obituary as "a keen golfer, an amusing raconteur and an ardent party-goer who enjoyed fast cars and pretty women. He was never anything but colourful." His Edwardian mannerisms apparently attracted Veronica and they were clearly kindred spirits.

Articles about the garden, each accompanied by beautiful photographs, began to appear in local newspapers, in books and in magazines. The garden had been established for over twenty years, and had reached mature beauty. Veronica's daughter-in-law, Olda FitzGerald, had an article about the garden published in the American magazine *House and Garden* in March 1986. The Canadian magazine *Western Living* published an article in May of that year. A chapter on the garden was included in *In a Canadian Garden*, by Nicole Eaton and Hilary Weston, published in 1989.

"A lot is given, a lot is demanded," Veronica would often say. She extolled noblesse oblige, the price paid for privilege. Veronica explained that money is a great responsibility. Money was a means to an end; it is only important if used for important things. "Not doing things for the sake of doing things," she said, but doing things that "make the world a better place." Veronica saw the garden as her important contribution to the world. She opened the garden to the community on several occasions. She also began a passionate campaign to save the garden for perpetuity. As an aris-

Veronica (right) with Mary
Soames (second from right).

tocrat, she was acutely aware of the past and the future. She clearly
saw herself as custodian of the garden, a place to be enjoyed in the
present but preserved for the future. She was anxious to find a way
of preserving the garden, as well as her lifestyle.

Her church, St. Mark's Anglican, held social events in the garden. She had several art garden parties in support of the Old
School House in Qualicum and various garden groups, notably the
Mount Arrowsmith Rhododendron Society. The summer 1990
garden club newsletter describes a wine and dessert party held in
Veronica's garden: Guests ambled down pathways in the warm
evening sun while the rhododendrons were in full glory.

The height of this rosy era was, without doubt, the visits of
her many exalted guests. Her cousin Mary Soames, Winston
Churchill's daughter, visited the garden in May 1984. Lady Soames
was in western Canada on an eleven-day speaking engagement in
her role as patron of the Churchill Society. Veronica held a cocktail

party for her in the studio and arranged a tour of a forested park, Cathedral Grove, west of Qualicum. The absolute high points of this epoch, however, were the visits of royalty. Charles and Diana visited in 1986 and the Queen and Prince Philip in 1987.

Money once again became an on-going issue. When Veronica came to Qualicum, the Milners had had a great deal of money. Before the ownership of the property was transferred to Malaspina University-College in 1996, Veronica was, she told me, "nearly bankrupt." She had few liquid assets and a huge tax debt, she said. Servants, even those who were poorly paid and overworked, were costly. She continued to travel, and had expensive tastes. She was also generous to Desmond and Olda at Glin whenever possible.

Veronica juggled her desire to support an extravagant lifestyle with a wish to preserve the garden for the future. Over time, she became desperate about her financial situation. She did not have Ray's ability to generate capital. She sold many of her jewels, pieces of furniture and art. She also sold several pieces of land she and Ray had purchased in the area. At times, she invited people to the garden, then, at the end of the day, asked them for $2, in an inept effort at fund-raising. There are countless stories that she failed to pay her bills in local shops. Several of her friends recall that Veronica made excessive demands on both their time and their wallets. For example, she did not expect to pick up the bill for things such as restaurant meals.

Veronica did not substantially curtail her travelling, and frequently visited Glin. There would be a great commotion before she arrived, as all of her personal possessions would have been put away. Una, her personal maid, had returned to live in Ireland and always took care of Veronica's belongings. They would be laid out just so before her arrival. Veronica would arrive and everything would be "beautiful" for a day or two, Tom Wall recalled. It was a honeymoon period. "Then she got down to business." Veronica had always stayed in the "pink room" overlooking the Shannon. Although the family had moved into the wing, in order to make a success of the hotel, Veronica would remain in the main house and talk to the guests, even when it became awkward or embarrassing. Veronica never liked to be alone, and would put great demands on the family and staff to sit with her. She invited friends from England, entertained her old local friends, and those she felt would be of some benefit to her. She kept the door open to the kitchen until company came. She took, Tom recalled, a "terrible interest in everything" and never accepted that she was no longer in charge. "You never knew when she was go-ing to leave," Tom said. "She would change her mind ten times and you would never really be sure until she drove down the driveway."

A favourite spot at Glin.

Veronica would always spend a day or two in the garden at Glin, moving from place to place on a portable seat while Tom worked. She would keep a table close to the window so "she could spot any problem first hand. Suddenly she would call and you would have to drop everything and come straight on," Tom reported. She took a special interest in the walled garden, and items she may have left in the greenhouse. From time to time, she still loved to prune fruit trees espaliered along in the garden wall.

Her home, however, was now permanently in Qualicum Beach where she grappled with future prospects. One of Veronica's few solutions to her financial problems would have been to find another wealthy husband. Even late in life, Veronica was an attractive woman and had many male admirers. For some time she was very intent on remarriage. A relative once scolded her:

[He] has nothing to offer in such backgrounds as Ireland and London, where you are most in tune. Ray was only welcome because he was such an exceptionally nice man. Can't you try to interest yourself in your own life, as Aunt Elaine did and as I do? At present (and when I saw you) you were thinking about absolutely nothing except getting married — to one man or another!!!

For some time, she had a lover who lived in Victoria. Several friends described the way Veronica would "chase" the wealthy gentleman. She would travel to Victoria if he did not come to see her. His answer to her proposal: "Why don't we get married?" was firm. "No. I would be broke if we did."

Because of financial problems and Veronica's increasingly difficult and demanding nature, the garden began to decline. There was a high turnover of garden staff and less money to devote to the garden. As a result, many fine specimens were lost. The rhododendrons, which form an understorey to the forest, suffered from a lack of light as the forest matured, just as Ted Grieg had feared. When the local art gallery, The Old School House, had a fundraising event in the garden, volunteers spent weeks cleaning up in preparation. The task became so onerous, a new location had to be found for future events.

Subdivisions sprang up in Qualicum Beach. In Veronica's mind, they were "common" affairs with clipped lawns and antiseptic sameness. One of the tracts of land she sold was subdivided and named "Chartwell," apparently in honour of Churchill's estate in England. It may have been a coincidence, or perhaps even meant as a compliment, that the subdivision was named for Veronica's famous relation. Veronica told me, however, she felt the subdivision had been named as a personal insult to her.

Despite her abhorrence of subdivisions in general, Veronica had several schemes to sell or subdivide herself. In late fall, 1977, she had Nanaimo land surveyor Charles Smythies draw up plans for the proposed subdivision of the property. Veronica received support for this project from her brother Amherst. He wrote to her:

I am very glad that you have gone ahead with the survey to know the value of the property if subdivided efficiently because it will always stand you in good stead as and when you sell even if the new owner decides to keep it all intact . . .

She again corresponded with Smythies in 1982 via her lawyer. Subdivision was still a possibility and this time, the project seemed more likely to proceed. A third party proposed purchasing the property rather than have it subdivided. The idea fell flat when it became clear that the town would require road access through adjoining properties, something Veronica knew neighbours would never agree to. In the mid-1980s, the town of Qualicum Beach established "estate residential" zoning for the old-growth properties

View from the house.

where Veronica's garden sits. The bylaw prohibited the subdivision of the properties into lots smaller than two and a half acres, and effectively put an end to Veronica's plans.

Veronica had a video made in the 1980s. In it, she describes the development of the garden. "Few had the time, energy or money to make places like this," she said. While the rest of Canada was being "developed into squares," rising assessments and taxes were making it impossible to keep her garden intact for future generations. She went on to say that she had visited a great many botanical gardens on her travels. Her hope was that the garden could be preserved, perhaps for a "school of horticulture." In yet another plan, she envisioned the establishment of a school of fine arts in Qualicum Beach, perhaps along the lines of the Banff School of Fine Arts.

Veronica considered selling the property several times and certainly received encouragement from friends to do this. Her long-time friend Lillian urged her: "Although it can take ages to sell very valuable property, I think you should put Long Distance on the market. It will become less and less suited to you as the years go by, and is useless to Desmond when you die…"

In March 1986, Veronica met with the Premier of British Columbia, Bill Vander Zalm, to discuss a possible development of the garden, perhaps in line with his own Fantasy Garden World. Vander Zalm's $7 million garden extravaganza was located south of Vancouver. It featured a miniature railway, large statues and a miniature castle relocated from the Expo 86 site. It also had a strong biblical theme. The garden included a miniature River Jordan and Sea of Galilee. The children's area included a replica of Noah's ark with a tape-recorded story of the great flood. It appears that Vander Zalm's vision for Veronica's garden would follow a similar path. Vander Zalm wrote:

The basic concept would be to develop further your beautiful garden so as to make it THE CENTRE OF ARTS *in North America. You should consider featuring both audio and visual arts. Part of the identity for the garden should be many displays of statues or busts of famous artists and composers in beautifully landscaped floral surrounding.*

Vander Zalm explained that he was not in a position to make a financial contribution, as his own resources were already committed. A limited company should be formed including himself, Veronica and a "third party to provide the funding."

Veronica visited Fantasy Gardens with the Vander Zalms and developed a friendly relationship with them. It is, however, hard to imagine Veronica carrying through with such a venture. Although she would have been attracted to his conservative politics, Veronica was not a populist. While he had some status as premier of the province, Vander Zalm is Dutch, one of the many ethnic groups she professed to despise. Her Victorian and artistic sensibilities made the idea of commercialism repugnant. Veronica preferred a radically different style of garden. She had an abhorrence of what she called "vulgarity," and Vander Zalm's garden was certainly very different from her own. Above all, he had no money to contribute to the venture.

One of Veronica's more persistent

Magnolias.

ideas was the formation of a "National Trust" for Canada. It was a reincarnation of her plans to preserve Glin before her marriage to Ray. She wrote letters to politicians including federal Heritage Minister Sheila Copps. The Queen, Veronica wrote, had agreed that a National Trust for Canada was long overdue. Copps responded several months later. She claimed that she shared Veronica's concerns, but could only offer vague reassurances. The government was examining tax measures, she wrote, that would be advantageous to the restoration and preservation of historical sites.

Veronica wrote to one of Ray's former business associates:

We are beseeched [sic] from within [Canada] with sell-out forces — big business; real estate developers; highway departments. . .all in collusion with federal, provincial and local government departments intent upon taxing our hearths and lands out of existence. . . . It is time to found a National Trust of Canada on the English lines. After the first world war, the English National Trust saved England from being cut up and sold down the river by real estate developers in cahoots with government departments.

The National Trust ended the appalling power of these people.

Veronica saw Prince Charles as a likely patron or protector of the garden. She wrote to him several times seeking his involvement in preserving the garden. In 1989 she wrote:

Three years have passed since your visit to Long Distance and as the years go by, I am becoming increasingly concerned about its future well-being. It is my wish to preserve this place as a bird sanctuary, botanical garden and arburitum [sic]. . . . It occurs to me that you might like to have a very secluded, private residence for you and your family. Your guardianship would provide a safe haven for the garden and its inhabitants for future generations to enjoy.

She negotiated unsuccessfully with two large universities in British Columbia, the University of British Columbia and the University of Victoria. In 1992, The University of Victoria, under President David Strong, proposed the establishment of an "International Centre for the Study of Global Change" at the site. Scientists, businessmen, politicians and educators could gather in the serene surroundings of the garden to reflect on environmental problems. Although they held out hope for several years, in the end the university was not able to raise the money that the proposal required.

The estate was put up for sale in 1992. The episode illustrated Veronica's ambivalence and conflicted thinking. *Vancouver Sun* reporter Moira Farrow wrote an article about what she called "a must-see for mansion buyers." The estate had been listed for three or four weeks and the Victoria-based realtor was quoted as saying there had been a great deal of interest in it. Veronica, however, began to waiver. The reporter noted:

...whether the house...is really for sale is questionable. Even though [the realtor] talked about the listing, the 83 year-old owner, Veronica Milner, said in an interview...she has decided not to sell it after all. "I just took it off the market," she said. "I had thought of selling it but I changed my mind. I change my mind every day. It isn't for sale at the moment but it could be in the future."

Still, the need for money clashed with her passion to preserve the garden and forest. In 1995, she hired a logging company that removed a large number of trees from the property, including large, old specimens. The operation only came to an end when the town, at the urging of neighbours, passed a bylaw preventing the cutting or removal of any tree over three metres in height. Veronica was

Tom Wall with the
pine at Glin.

eighty-six years old when this piece of logging took place. One aspect of the adventure worth noting is that she continued to plan her garden. As a part of the logging operation, an area was roughed out and water diverted to a pond that, she hoped, would become a Japanese garden. Funds prevented this from completion, but she was still thinking of projects to develop the garden to a further stage. This was also typical of how she viewed the garden at Glin. Tom Wall shook his head as he described "pine" trees she planted at Glin when she was in advanced years "You begin to wonder how she expected to see them grow," he said to me. "There was no end in sight to her vision" for the garden.

Despite the increasing pressures, life continued according to the garden's own particular rhythm. Afternoon tea with cakes and sweets. Before-dinner drinks were typically gin and tonic or a Bloody Mary with spicy nuts and bolts, sometimes accompanied by sandwiches. Dinner was served in the formal dining room lit by candles in an alabaster porcelain candelabra. Dinner was typically soup, followed by roast lamb, chicken or salmon, roasted potatoes and vegetables such as asparagus or carrots. Pudding and cake for dessert might lead to cheese and grapes, chocolate and coffee. On special nights, guests still retired to the drawing room for coffee in demitasse oriental cups.

The house was now becoming rather run-down, yet the table was always set with botanical place mats from the Dublin Irish Georgian Society that her son was very involved with. A silver bowl filled with seasonal flowers was invariably on the table: spring daffodils, summer roses, hydrangeas in early fall, rose hips and shrubs with colourful winter berries or foliage at Christmas. Place cards were in order for formal dinner parties. A small brass bell

Interior.

was at Veronica's right hand, ready to summon the help from the kitchen.

An extremely sensuous person, Veronica could gaze at the evening sun and the darkening evening sky in utter tranquillity. She loved the taste and smell of food and wine and chocolate. She enjoyed music, with speakers in the drawing room and dining room; music filled the air during dinner. She also loved silence: "the sound of no sound."

Veronica lived surrounded by flowers. There were flowers on the walls, in her paintings, on cushions and ornaments. The drawing room was able to seat twenty, its chairs arranged for conversation.

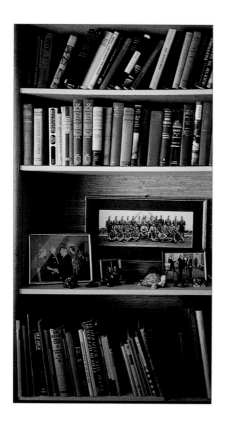

Top: Books and photos in the studio;
above: Veronica's cluttered private study;
right: drawing room.

Like the rest of the house, the room was bursting with flowers arranged under Veronica's practised eye.

In later days and in the style of "old money," and endorsed by Queen Victoria, everything became a little shabby. The Queen had hated "vulgarity," preferring the relatively low-key, well worn and comfortable. These became symbolic of "old" money and "old" families. Not only should an item be used as long as possible, but if it were a little ragged it meant you had had it long enough to get that way. It was a way to differentiate one from the nouveau riche. Veronica's view was similar. The house and contents became time-worn and tired-looking, but retained an aura of remembered elegance.

Beautifully produced books on gardens, Ireland and the monarchy filled the coffee table and bookshelves. In spring, fall and winter, a fire crackled in the sitting room, although on pleasant days the outer door would be propped open by a painted rock to let in the fresh outside air.

Veronica was especially fond of dogs. She believed that dogs know all about us. "They understand everything we say and can even read our thoughts," she said. She explained that she loved dogs in order to have another living being to touch. Veronica believed dogs know "more than humans about everything that goes on." She was enchanted with a children's movie, *Fluke*, in which a man's soul inhabits a dog and becomes the family pet to his grieving family.

In later years, the dogs of choice were Cavalier King Charles Spaniels, long-time favourites in royal and aristocratic circles. According to psychologist Stanley Coren, Queen Victoria, Charles I, Charles II, King James and Mary, Queen of Scots had all owned them. The Duchess of Marlborough kept them. The breed was named after King Charles II, to whom Veronica's relation Barbara Villiers, was mistress. Charles was so fond of the breed that he commissioned a ceiling mural of them in his bedroom. Veronica often remarked that the breed of dog was given a royal charter allowing them to roam "without let or hindrance" anywhere in the British Isles.

Veronica's first King Charles Spaniels were Tara and Sesu. Sesu, an Icelandic name, was suggested by her friend Joan Magnusson.

Painting of native plants by Veronica Milner.

Tara, the favourite, had puppies on St. Patrick's Day. Veronica got up in the night to watch the puppies' birth, and was amazed and delighted by the six newborns. Later she took photos of the black and white pups frolicking in the garden.

While her Irish dogs are remembered with plaques on stone walls of the inner courtyard at Glin, Tara and Sesu are buried in the garden under a pyramidal gravestone near the house in Qualicum.

Willow, the last of her beloved King Charles Spaniels, was old when Veronica purchased her. She had been a breeding dog and had had several litters before retiring into luxury. The dog was pampered and indulged. Willow ate cookies at teatime and seemed to have an internal clock that knew precisely when tea was to be served. At dinner, she was served a portion on her own small plate brought into the dining room and presented to Veronica for her approval before being fed to the dog.

Veronica continued a lifelong love of birds. Seeds were hung over windows. Trays of water were set out under bushes. At Glin, she insisted that birdfeeders be kept full in the walled garden near her favourite resting spot. At Qualicum, she loved to watch families of quail in spring. Veronica became a friend of the Victoria painter of birds Fenwick Lansdowne. On one visit, Lansdowne reportedly recorded forty-eight different songbirds in the garden area.

Over time, Qualicum continued to change. It became less British. Many of the old soldiers and remittance men had died and a great influx of retirees arrived from the mainland and eastern Canada. Old friends like Mary Greig passed away. Parksville to the south became a strip mall of fast food places and motels. The garden remained a haven of tranquillity, an oasis protected from the world that was increasingly intruding with demands for higher taxes and with new ideas about roles and behaviour. Veronica's garden possessed the charm of an earlier era, reminders of Victorian England and the British Empire. It became for Veronica her last link to another time and way of life.

CHAPTER EIGHT

Royal Visitors

Twilight and evening bell
And after that the dark!
And may there be no sadness of farewell,
When I embark.

— Alfred, Lord Tennyson

CHARLES AND DIANA opened Expo 86 in Vancouver, amid incessant flashing cameras, frenzied press, and speeding motorcades. The gruelling schedule of appearances marks the work of royalty. The royal visit to Canada lasted from April 30 until May 7 and included visits to Victoria, Vancouver, Prince George, Kamloops and Nanaimo, British Columbia. Charles and Diana opened the $1.6 billion world fair, launched an art festival, went to the opera and symphony, dedicated parks, rode Vancouver's new Sky-Train, sailed on a B.C. ferry, attended civic events, were welcomed to Canada at the provincial legislature and city halls. They cruised the Expo site by water and monorail and quickly toured seven pavilions. They attended official receptions, met mayors and premiers. Police held back excited crowds, eager to catch even the slightest glimpse of the future king and the glamorous and beautiful princess. The crowd was too polite to push, but anxious and excited enough to press against police barricades.

Veronica, Charles and Diana in the dining room.

At about 10:30 A.M. on May 5, turmoil erupted on the beach below the garden at Qualicum as Charles and Diana arrived by plane and were transported to shore by hovercraft. Even Diana mentioned how it must have seemed like an invasion. The din peaked while two larger vessels, a helicopter and a second hovercraft kept watch. In contrast, the grounds were full of silent security. Mobile police units hid in the bush with such skill "you couldn't even see them," said Veronica's friend Joan Magnusson.

The Royals were dressed casually. Charles wore a red windbreaker against the early spring cold. Both he and Diana wore slacks, while Veronica and her friends wore blouses and skirts. In Veronica's garden, the couple had a break from the rigours of the road. The garden offered a refuge where they could relax for a few hours. Both wandered through the garden, at its peak of glorious colour in May. Their day in Qualicum was the only "private" part of the Canadian tour.

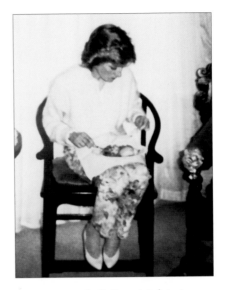

Left: (left to right) Arthur Erickson, Veronica, Charles, Hilary Weston, Diana, Galen Weston.

According to well-laid plans, fresh orange juice was ready. The day was cold and blustery, however, and the careful plans had to be quickly changed. Instead of orange juice, the party requested coffee. Veronica waited in the rain to greet the party while Raju, a servant, was dispatched in haste to prepare hot drinks. The party included Diana's lady-in-waiting Anne Beckwith-Smith, Galen and Hilary Weston, Charles' private secretary David Roycroft, Veronica's secretary, her friend Joan Magnusson and Desmond's old friend Arthur Erickson, the architect, much to Veronica's annoyance.

Lunch was served in the dining room, precisely at one. Not a minute before, or after. Veronica had arranged a hot and cold buffet, no doubt planned to perfection. They ate sitting casually in the dining room, plates balanced on laps. Diana's feet were hooked into the rung of a Chinese chair. She wore pink flowered pants; her soft pink sweater buttoned up the front.

Rhododendron "May Day" in bloom.

Charles and Diana seemed relaxed and happy. Veronica was at her best in the role of wonderful hostess, charming and attentive to her guests' needs. She had a lively discussion with Charles, with whom she shared many interests, including gardens and painting. Diana, never known as a brilliant conversationalist, was, Veronica recalled, "charming," but less talkative. Joan Magnusson described the visit as being remarkably normal. Charles drew in his sketch-book, while Diana sat in the drawing room and on the veranda. They walked in the garden. Even in the mist and rain, the spring garden would have been glorious, with blossoms still clinging to the masses of camellias, rhododendrons and azaleas up the drive and around the veranda. The red rhododendron May Day put on her yearly show below the drawing room window.

By four o'clock it was over. They exchanged gifts, including signed photographs from Charles and Diana. They signed the guest book, Diana drawing a childish happy face beneath her name. Charles left by boat, while Diana left by a different route.

That night, back in Vancouver, Diana and Charles both wrote thank you notes in their own hand to Veronica after they returned to the Pan Pacific Hotel. Diana's letter showed a remarkable kindness and empathy, extraordinary from a person rumoured to be spoiled and most certainly used to being "treated like royalty."

Dear Veronica:

It was so very kind of you to have had us in your home today — what a break for us to come & have a peaceful day away from it all in such wonderful surroundings.

You'd obviously gone to enormous trouble to make our visit a happy one & we did enjoy ourselves more than you can possibly imagine.

Our lunch was delicious & it was such a relief to sit down quietly without looking at a watch before rushing off again in a car & getting ghastly indigestion!!

The surroundings of your home were so beautiful — All those different flowers & trees made us feel as though we were back in England & I can so see that you love it as we do.

Our arrival must have felt like an invasion, but I did just want you to know how deeply we appreciated your kindness & what a difference it has made to this particular couple having had a magical day with you.

This comes with my warmest possible wishes.

Yours Sincerely,
Diana

Although Diana indeed seemed sincere, there was an interesting aside to this letter. Diana fainted at Expo the day after she visited Veronica in Qualicum. She had gone out of her way to mention the food, how delicious it was, and that it was a change from her normal digestive problems. Biographer Andrew Morton claimed that Diana had not eaten since the flight to Vancouver from England and even then she had only a piece of chocolate bar aboard the plane!

History now reveals that Diana had suffered from bulimia since her engagement and had made several suicide attempts. The marriage was strained by the shadow of Charles' continued relationship with Camilla Parker-Bowles and by the press and public adoration of Diana. In retrospect, there were signs in Vancouver that things were not well. When they attended the symphony, photographers asked Charles if he could move aside so they could get a clear photograph of Diana. The *Province* newspaper quotes him as saying "What do you want me to do? Step backwards, step forwards or stand on my head?" The paper reported, "No one replied."

Morton claimed that his book *Diana, Her True Story* was based on interviews tape-recorded at Kensington Palace in 1991. By 1986, the marriage was already rocky. The revised edition of Morton's book, released a month after Diana's death in 1997, contained transcripts of the tapes upon which the first edition was based. The transcripts included Diana's description of the trip to Expo:

We'd been walking round for four hours, we hadn't had any food and presumably I hadn't eaten for days beforehand. When I say that, I mean food staying down. I remember walking round feeling really ghastly. I didn't tell anyone I felt ghastly because I thought they'd think I was whinging. I put my arm on my husband's shoulder and said: 'Darling, I think I'm about to disappear,' and slid down the side of him.

She claimed the fainting angered Charles:

My husband told me off. He said I could have passed out quietly somewhere else, behind a door. It was all very embarrassing. My argument was I didn't know anything about fainting.

She recalled that she was "overtired, exhausted." This is likely very true, given the gruelling schedule. It must have been obvious to at least some that the situation was strained. At least two local newspapers noted that an RCMP officer waved waiting reporters and photographers away from the Royals, saying, "Go way! They need a break."

Diana's statement about not having eaten for days may have been due to confusion about the chronology of events after such a long passage of time. It is also possible, of course, that she vomited her Qualicum lunch, or that the whole situation was exaggerated. In any case, it seems clear that she enjoyed a break at Qualicum from the vigorous tour days in the public eye.

Charles also expressed gratitude for the peaceful, relaxing change of scene. He wrote:

Vancouver   May 5th 1986

Dear Veronica:

A thousand thanks for such a peaceful day — and your company, even though I know you said I shouldn't thank you! It was a wonderful escape to sanity and botany & I did enjoy myself — aided of course by the ubiquitous "Bloody Veronicas!" You must be very proud of your garden after all these years & I too think those Douglas firs are magnificent trees. I had no idea they were as old as you said.

Lunch was a memorable affair & utterly delicious, & we felt very spoilt to be looked after so beautifully.

It made such a difference to my life to be able to do a little drawing before and after lunch. It is the best therapy I know — but I am preaching to the converted!

As we returned in the boat from Howe Sound this afternoon the sun came out — it would! — and no doubt tomorrow will be a lovely day... However, we have masses of happy, sunny memories of your generosity & send renewed gratitude & warmest regards —

Yours most sincerely

Charles

Back at Qualicum on the day of the visit, the phone started to ring at six. Reporters had been looking everywhere for the Royals and some intrepid journalist made a good guess. Charles was spotted en route to Vancouver. After a time, Veronica tired of the reporters and took the phone off the hook. As soon as the line was re-established at eleven that night, the phone rang again. The London press was calling, wanting details of the visit. The persistence of the press was "a shock to me," Joan recalled.

According to Veronica, Charles and Diana had been "very much in love" during their visit to the garden. When intense rumours began to appear in the press later that year about the unhappy state of the marriage, Veronica was shocked. Despite the events of the next few years, she was proud that she had been able to give the Prince of Wales and his princess peace and privacy for even one day.

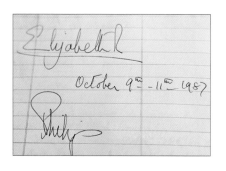

Queen Elizabeth and Prince Philip visited the garden from October 9 to 11, 1987. I asked Veronica how it came to be that she had such exalted visitors. She told me that it was because one of her relations had been an important member of the Queen's household. While it seems very likely that this may have played a role, a more likely scenario is that the visit was arranged through Galen and

Hilary Weston. The very wealthy Westons are good friends of Charles. Dublin-born Hilary, lieutenant-governor of Ontario, has an interest in gardens and Veronica's garden is featured in the book *In a Canadian Garden*, co-authored by Weston. Perhaps Charles confirmed to his parents that the garden was lovely and Veronica hospitable.

Neither the Queen nor Philip were strangers to Canada nor to Qualicum. This was the Queen's fourteenth official visit to Canada. As mentioned earlier, the Queen and Prince Philip had stayed at Eaglecrest, a very short distance from the Milner estate. The Queen had also visited Nanaimo several times. On March 10, 1983, the Queen and Prince Philip visited Nanaimo aboard the royal yacht *Britannia*. Their itinerary included a stop at the campus of Malaspina College.

A royal visit, especially one by the Queen over two nights, involves elaborate preparation. Documents arrive in advance with royal requirements and preferences. Notes go to the Queen about the communities and dignitaries she is to visit. Every aspect from personal comfort to protection must be perfect.

Buckingham Palace had approached hotel owner Leo Teijgeman and his wife Susan of the local Old Dutch Inn. For a month, the Teijgemans planned every detail from menus to laundry and housekeeping details. Even plans for the disposal of royal garbage had to be made. Protocol officers visited "Long Distance" in July and again in September. The British Columbia Building Corporation (BCBC) did its part by painting the master bedroom; all vestiges and belongings of Veronica's were removed from the clothes closets for the duration of the visit. Even a new mattress was installed for the Queen.

Columnist Jim Gibson reported that the government graded the driveway, installed a flagpole for the royal insignia, cleaned the roof and gutters, and washed windows. The garden was spruced up, the boiler and water system serviced, carpets cleaned and tacked. A new stovetop was installed in the kitchen, even though food was prepared at the kitchens of the Old Dutch Inn and transported to the house by van.

As a part of both Royal visits, elaborate security measures were set in place. Well before the big day, RCMP photographers from the forensic lab arrived on the scene. On both occasions the photographer was a female officer who described herself as being "young and impressionable" at the time. She had recently joined the force, and recalled that Veronica herself opened the door. Veronica accompanied the RCMP in the helicopter while the site was photographed from every possible angle. Afterward, she led the police on a tour of the garden. No doubt this was a radical departure from the usual gruesome tasks of forensic photography. "I'll never forget her," the officer told me.

When Charles and Diana visited, the event was a closely guarded secret. Joan Magnusson recalled: "We had to keep silent for three months. One little slip and it would be out." When the Queen and Prince Philip visited the next year, things were very different. The proposed stay was announced beforehand, but was a "private visit," leaving the royal couple in total privacy. This meant even privacy from Veronica. Security was much more intense. Only the Teijge-mans and Veronica's household staffs were able to cross the elaborate security lines surrounding the house. The day before the visit, Veronica and Joan Magnusson moved to the Old Dutch Inn along with Veronica's dogs. Several members of the Queen's entourage, including her personal secretary, also stayed at the Inn.

Veronica was featured on the front pages of both the *Vancouver Sun* and the *Victoria Times-Colonist*. She told reporters that she hoped to be invited for tea, as "I have never met the Queen although I have met her father. I met the prince at Banff School of Fine Arts years ago."

The 1987 visit took place during one of those autumns when summer lingered on. Each sunny, golden day was a gift. Cold, damp nights crept up and temperatures were slow to rise, but afternoons were streaked with golden hues and unseasonable warmth. No bitter winds or thick grey rain had yet broken the thread from summer. The air smelled of fall as plants prepared for winter. A rare white eucryphia was lovely with white flowers. The trees had started their transformation to radiant shades of crimson, purple and yellow. Roses and dahlias were still in full flower.

The sun shone as the royal couple landed in Victoria before heading to Qualicum on a chartered Air BC Dash-7. Looking splendid in an emerald green outfit and matching pillbox hat, the Queen greeted adoring crowds during the fifteen-minute stopover. Canadian Governor General Jeanne Sauvé, Prime Minister Brian Mulroney and assorted politicians welcomed her.

Gibson said in his Victoria column, "Somehow it's hard to imagine the Royals out on the lawn, with the briquettes aglow, arguing whether the bangers need more time on the barbie." Yet, Philip did indeed barbecue. He swam in the garden's solar-heated pool and chatted amiably with the help. The Queen enjoyed the tranquillity of the autumn garden, birds and roses.

The Queen also had a great deal to prepare for the rigorous days to come at the 5-day, $19 million Commonwealth Heads of Government conference in Vancouver. All was not well in the commonwealth. Military dictatorships ruled many of the member countries. A recent overthrow in Fiji was on the top of the agenda. Before the conference, Amnesty International released a report accusing thirty-three of the forty-nine Commonwealth countries, including Britain and India, of serious violations of human rights including beatings, torture and use of excessive force. Several countries supported the imposition of economic sanctions against South Africa. Other problems such as AIDS and illicit drugs were to be addressed.

At the same time, the royal family was under increasing personal stress. The rift between Charles and Diana had become much more public and obvious. For example, they met only once in five weeks during that autumn. The Queen's son Andrew and daughter-in-law Sarah, the Duke and Duchess of York, were also causing headlines. They were seen in the company of pop singer Boy George and a former brothel keeper. There was a noticeable lack of British press present when the Queen and Prince Philip arrived in Canada, many preferring to stay at home and follow the sensational personal drama unfolding there. Martin Bell of the British Broadcasting Corporation noted, "The Queen isn't news any more – her children are."

Veronica got her wish to meet the Queen. On the last day of the two-and-a-half day visit, she was invited for tea an hour before the couple was set to leave. Veronica had a "last minute inspiration to have a tree" in memory of the visit. The Queen planted a Spanish chestnut in what is now known as the Queen's garden. Philip planted a maple. As there was, Veronica felt, "no room left in the garden," the tree is planted outside the garden gates.

It is customary for royal visitors to leave gifts for their hosts — signed photo-

The Queen planted a tree outside the garden gate.

graphs, small tokens for each of the staff and servants. The Queen gave Veronica a red, leather-bound two-volume book entitled *Royal Heritage,* signed Elizabeth R, 1987. Veronica added, "Given to Mrs. Veronica Milner at "Long Distance" Qualicum Beach, Vancouver Island, BC before she attended the Commonwealth Conference 1987 (when she visited the house for 2½ days before Vancouver — Oct. 1987)." Veronica and a guest were invited to dine with the Queen at the Premier's dinner in Vancouver on October 15.

Veronica told me that talking to the Queen was "just like talking to you." The Queen apparently reported that she felt "very at home," in part because there were family pictures in the sitting room, framed copies of photographs taken during Charles and Diana's visit the year before.

While the visit was a coup for Veronica, it was also disappointing. The visit marked a final separation from some people in Qualicum that Veronica had known for several years. In Veronica's view, several of the more "tiresome" Qualicum matrons were beside themselves with jealousy. Some of the press coverage had not been flattering to Veronica and she was greatly inconvenienced by the visit. A friend of Veronica's told me she remarked to her that the Queen had treated her rather badly. Veronica paused for a moment and then replied: "Yes, I suppose she did."

Late summer, on an August evening in 1997 the sky was deep blue with only a few high clouds. The hydrangeas were in bloom and the maple trees had started to turn colour. The fragrant glorybower tree, *Clerodendrun trichotomum*, rare and borderline to the region, was in bloom. It produced sprays of starlike flowers, swelling from green to pink to white. A magnolia was in second bloom; its soft petals blush pink. The golden plum and apple trees were becoming heavy with fall fruit.

Clerodendrun trichotomun (Glorybower tree).

Jim and I were sitting on the veranda looking at photos of the garden with Veronica when the telephone rang. Diana, Princess of Wales, had been in a terrible car accident. Her boyfriend, Dodi Fayed, also in the car, was dead. At the same time Linda, one of Veronica's "helpers," clearly upset, came from inside the house with a radio. Veronica grasped the radio and twisted the dial, attempting to turn up the volume but instead putting it off the station. "Turn that off," she snapped.

The evening air became misty white,

the ocean green. Shafts of light shot through the gathering clouds as the sky turned red. Long shadows crept across the lawn and the hills turned golden, then violet. The wind in the trees was like a small silver wave. At one point, Veronica stunned us by announcing, "I'm glad. They didn't deserve her." We sat in silence, listening to the birds, watching the sky slowly darken.

"I love the sound of no sound," she said.

From time to time, Veronica would reminisce about Diana's visit to the garden. "She sat there," Veronica said, pointing to the other end of the veranda.

"Imagine living like that," apparently referring to the press and paparazzi who had pursued Diana.

"She'll be okay," she commented as the changing wind stirred the waves on the beach. The surf slapped the shells and slid back into the sea.

"Charles painted in the garden for an hour," she recalled as the sky turned deeper blue.

"*That Woman,*" apparently in reference to Camilla Parker-Bowles, "should be exiled," she said as clouds overhead rippled into a mackerel sky.

After a time she commented, "The Prince of Wales will never be king." A silver vapour trail diffused into nothing, blown by some high wind.

As the evening wore on, Veronica said, "There is a darkness in the garden tonight." She pulled her sweater tight against a sudden touch of cold. Finally, there was only blackness and the sound of waves on the shore. "She has escaped it and the boys will be safe now," she sighed.

We sat in the dark until Linda came out again. "It's not good…" she began. Veronica cut her off and turned to me. "Will you stay with me and hold my hand?" she asked as she eased herself up from the chair to go in to the television. "This will be the worst part."

Veronica's first response, in the confusion and disbelief at the confirmation of Diana's death, appeared to be relief. "It would have been a muddle forever," she mumbled as we watched the CBC news report. Willow, the dog, jumped onto Veronica's lap as Peter Mansbridge and reporter Don Murray in London discussed the "pitiful" car chase. The pictures of the crumpled car in the tunnel played again and again. "Dreadful." Veronica joined in to the sombre comments of the newscasters.

Veronica was anxious that we stay, finding excuses to keep us from leaving even though we had early morning obligations. She asked me to take photographs of a photograph of Diana and herself, a reassurance of some permanence, at least, of memories.

On Saturday, September 6, 1997, a memorial service was held for Diana in St. Mark's Church, Qualicum Beach. Veronica asked us to accompany her. The minister designed his service after many of the tributes that were broadcast around the world. While not full, the church held a fair number of people. A young girl placed flowers on the altar. Veronica sat with us halfway down the church on the right-hand side. After the service, we drove through Qualicum, and had lunch at the College Inn. Veronica had me pick up several copies of the newspaper that had an article about her response to Diana's death to send to the family in Ireland. We drafted the words to a memorial plaque for the garden that was never installed.

On Sunday, May 24, 1998, we picked up Veronica, loaded her into the car, and drove north on the new Island Highway to a nursery south of Courtenay. Before her death, the owner had ordered a rose named in honour of Princess Diana. Now that the unexpected had happened, he kindly set aside one of the now rare and coveted specimens for Veronica. She stayed in the car while we did an initial tour of the nursery. We then loaded her into her wheelchair. As we had tea on the cold patio, she pointed to several plants, water trays for birds and ceramic pots. "I'll have this and this," she would point at merchandise without bothering to ask the price as the bill mounted ever higher. She chose several Harkness roses imported from England. Soon Veronica's purchases got to the point that special arrangements had to be made to ship the goods by truck to Qualicum.

That same spring, Charles and his sons visited British Columbia. Once again, they were visiting the Westons. The boys enjoyed a few days of skiing at Whistler. I asked Veronica if she hoped to hear from the Prince of Wales. She replied: "He doesn't bother with me, so why should I bother with him?"

While Veronica's contacts with the royals were not always as extensive or as long-lasting as she might have wished, she remained a staunch monarchist for the rest of her life and was disturbed by any suggestion of the collapse of ancient institutions.

CHAPTER NINE

Saving the Garden

Had I the heavens' embroidered cloths,
Enwrought with golden and silver light,
The blue and the dim and the dark cloths
Of night and light and the half light,
I would spread the cloths under your feet:
But I, being poor, have only my dreams;
I have spread my dreams under your feet;
Tread softly because you tread on my dreams.

— W.B. Yeats

VERONICA WAS increasingly anxious to preserve her garden. She was growing older, and money was tight. She had to balance the twin problems of maintaining her lifestyle and preserving the garden for future generations. Her financial situation was such that donating the garden to an organization was not an option. She would need to be compensated financially in any scheme she entered into. Plans with several universities had fallen through. Despite her pleading, no other organization was able to take on her property.

She continued to canvass anyone and everyone – her mission in life became saving the garden. Even the social and public events that took place in the garden were all seen in the context of making it more appealing. For example, Veronica was well aware that the royal visits gave the garden publicity and status. Later, she was instrumental in nominating Mary Greig for an honorary degree from the University of Victoria, an award granted posthumously on June 1, 1991. Some of those close to the situation felt that Veronica's motivation in promoting Mary's work was to enhance the appeal of the garden to a buyer.

Malaspina University-College opened in 1969 as Vancouver Island's first community college, in an old hospital building in Nanaimo with forty employees. Under the leadership of President Rich Johnston, it was transformed into a University-College, occupying a 110-acre site on the slopes of Mount Benson and with an employee complement of almost 2000. More importantly, it had obtained degree-granting status and was moving in new directions. A foundation board, in its infancy, was vital for fund-raising and was indicative of the tremendous community support the institution enjoyed.

By 1995, President Johnston, known for his entrepreneurial spirit, began to explore the possibilities of acquiring the Milner property. Ross Fraser, then Dean of Arts at Malaspina, had met Veronica in 1988 when her cousin, the Earl of Bessborough, became an honorary patron of *Shakespeare Plus*, a summer literary event at the University-College. The Frasers had been friends with Veronica ever since and played a role in Malaspina's efforts to secure the property, including introducing Veronica to Johnston. Before leaving for a business trip to Mexico with his good friend and Foundation Board chair Jon Lampman, in February 1996, Johnston wrote to Veronica:

You have my assurances that I will continue to work hard to find a way to fund the project from a combination of public and private sources. I am optimistic that we will be able to present you a final proposal within two weeks of my return from Mexico.

MUC President Rich Johnston and Veronica.

174

Qualicum mayor Jack Collins, Malaspina Board Chair Jane Gregory, Rich Johnston and Jon Lampman at the garden dedication on May 17, 1996.

Upon his return, Johnston and Lampman were able to pull together what had eluded many before them. The arrangement allowed Veronica to remain in the house and for Malaspina to preserve the garden. Further, they were able to accomplish this without University-College money in a time when the institution was suffering through reduced federal transfer payments for education and a freeze on tuition. "I was proud that Malaspina University-College worked with private interests and the community to find a way to endow the property," he told me. On Friday, May 17, 1996, about 200 people attended a dedication ceremony on the grand lawn of the estate. Rich Johnston was master of ceremonies. He was clearly pleased as he explained to the crowd that the total value of the property, an annuity to be paid to Veronica, and a small endowment to maintain the garden made the package the largest donation ever made to a community or university-college in the history of British Columbia.

For a time, Veronica caused havoc at the University-College.

Frantic for attention, and certain she should only deal with the "top," she persistently called the president. She told me that she was "IMPORTANT in capital letters" and expected to be treated as such. The president, burdened with the significant duties of his office, was getting incessant telephone calls from Veronica. In one, she complained that the black squirrels were chasing the brown squirrels and something must be done *immediately!*

Another emergency phone call from Veronica sounded the alarm that the chickadees were without water. She wanted to know what President Johnston was going to do about it. After Johnston made the comment that surely chickadees, being birds, could find water on their own, Veronica retorted that she had always set the sprinklers in the late afternoon and the birds enjoyed a shower or two. With a newly installed sprinkler system, Johnston asked Jim to adjust the timing of the sprinklers.

Unfortunately, this was to have dire consequences. Rather than choosing to have tea on the veranda at four, as was her custom, Veronica and her guests were enjoying a late tea in the garden, when suddenly the system turned on, spraying the group. This incident precipitated another call to the president's office. He replied, "I am sorry, Veronica, I thought you wanted to have water available for the chickadees. How was I to know that you would be taking tea that late in the afternoon? I will certainly look into it."

In the spring of 1996, Johnston, at Veronica's urging, invited the Prince of Wales to become the honorary Patron of the Garden. Commander Richard Aylard, the prince's personal secretary, wrote: "His Royal Highness has given careful consideration to" the request, "but has decided, with regret, that he must decline." The prince, it seems, was too heavily committed to take on the project. He would, Aylard wrote, be unable to devote any time to it. Veronica, however, had not finished with the prince. Although her garden now appeared to be safe, Veronica continued her campaign to form a National Trust in Canada. On September 4, 1996, she again wrote to Prince Charles. "There is," she wrote, "considerable urgency, as all over Canada irreplaceable heritage properties are being desecrated by rapid and thoughtless development."

Like the garden, the house was in decline. The furnace was a constant source of problems. The roof needed replacing or patching, the carpets were worn and discoloured. She made many demands that Malaspina could not afford to carry out. The University-College tried to pacify her, however, with repairs such as replacing aging gutters. By June, the situation had deteriorated to the point at which Johnston was forced to write to Veronica, "I wish to be contacted on matters related to the property management only through Mr. Cadwaladr and his committee."

During the first year, Jim and I got to know Veronica. Very little was done to the garden so that we could follow it through the season's surprises. Veronica felt it was vital to instruct Jim, as future custodian, about her garden. She showed him areas of wildness where the garden merges with the forest, in a kind of controlled neglect. The long grass of the meadow contrasts with the tall upright trees and trimmed formal grand lawn. Jim and Veronica agreed that paths would be mown, leaving the bulbs to flourish in a succession of wild flowers, periwinkle, violets, English daisy, buttercups, cyclamen, viola and spring bulbs, each coming and going in succession before the first cutting.

More than anything, Veronica explained her abhorrence of "vulgarity." Soon after the university-college's involvement with

"Vulgar" tulips planted near the front door.

the garden began, a local business donated a very large number of bulbs to the garden. Students distributed them in various places. Near the front door, a student planted a large grouping of red hybrid tulips. As we came out the door with Veronica, she looked at Jim, pointed to the tulips and said bluntly, "Do that again, and I'll kill you." (Jim was delighted when, after Veronica's death, he found a slide that clearly showed almost identical red tulips in the same bed many, many years before. Had it been Veronica's idea, or had some other unfortunate incurred her wrath?)

Jim began to take inventory of the many tasks needing attention. Fences were rotting; soft and black, they crumbled at a touch. Some were held together in places by plants and vines, ready to fall or topple. Others rocked precariously. Paths, once laid out to allow feet to saunter carelessly through the rhododendron glade, had become overgrown and finally, hidden. Water no longer flowed

The garden was in
a state of decline.

through stream ways; a film of green algae covered still ponds, giving a brilliant green backdrop to the Boy on the Dolphin. The irrigation system was a patchwork and unreliable. Deer readily breached the fence to feast on roses. A laurel hedge along the cliff-top had completely engulfed paths where children used to play.

An important task was to decide essential questions about the preservation of the garden. What is to be preserved? Clearly, the garden would be kept as a woodland garden, and the forest would remain intact as much as possible. A garden, however, is a growing and changing thing. As the two photographs which follow illustrate, it does not remain static. The photo on the left was taken in the early 1960s. Note the Douglas-fir and birch (*Betula pendula*) trees. The photo on the right was taken by Jim in the late 1990s. The trees have grown to such an extent that the area is hardly recognizable but for the fir and birch.

A garden is a growing
and changing thing.
These two photographs
show the same location.
The photograph above
was taken in the early
1960s, the one at the
right was taken in the
late 1990s.

Archival photo of pyramid cedars in the snow. Snow would destroy them many years later.

Which picture represents the garden? Of course, they both do. The plan must be to maintain the central characteristics of the garden through inevitable change.

One of the early tasks by Malaspina University-College was to selectively remove diseased and dangerous trees. As Ted Greig had predicted many years before, rhododendrons in the grove had grown leggy from lack of sunlight. With Jim's persuasion and an arborist's report to back him up, Veronica agreed to the selective removal of thirteen trees. We were extremely apprehensive about how the noise and disruption of the operation would affect Veronica. Remarkably, she coped well as huge crane trucks slid into place, removing 80-to-100-foot-high trees from the forest, opening windows of sunlight for the rhododendrons.

Some of the introduced trees, seen in photographs taken well before Veronica's time, were well beyond their prime. The orchard continued to produce pears, apples and golden plums but was choked and shaded by a border of tall, leaning unsightly pyramidal cedars. I was grateful when the snow destroyed one, convincing Veronica they should be removed. No doubt, the orchard breathed a sigh of relief as the air flowed more freely. Several peegee hydrangeas along the drive were starting to expire, their root systems declining and central cores pulpy with decay. Cuttings were carefully taken for propagation and the near-exhausted plants removed. Also within the first two years, English ivy that had grown so profuse it smothered the forest floor was removed. When light and air were introduced, trilliums, erythroniums (fawn lilies), hardy cyclamens, wood anemones and other naturalized bulbs were unleashed from the choking hold of the vines.

The summer days of 1996 were hot and dry. We would often drive to the garden in the evening and Jim would pull hoses and sprinklers from place to place watering the rhododendrons. We would then stop in for a quick chat with Veronica. An extensive renewal of the irrigation system became, in part, a learning task for students who replaced the old patchwork system.

Manpower was limited to student projects and a growing group of volunteers. Students work in the garden in the manner of European apprentices, by the rhythms and the tasks demanded of each season. They began to propagate cuttings of interesting or particularly precarious specimens and participated in yearly design and construction projects. The first such project was a redesign of the area in front of the gardener's cottage. The building had been put in use as a classroom and the grass at the entrance could not withstand student traffic. Veronica participated in the design selection and enjoyed meeting the students.

An advisory board was formed to decide the future direction of the garden and to grapple with the enormous tasks ahead, not the least of which was fundraising. What would the vision of the garden be? What should the mission statement be? How would the endowment be maintained? What would happen to the house? Short and long-term goals needed to be developed. This group went on a retreat to the Bloedel Reserve on Bainbridge Island near Seattle at Easter 1998 to grapple with some of these questions.

Tours were arranged to gauge the impact of crowds. How could crowds be accommodated while preserving the garden? What safety measures would have to be taken? Early openings had a makeshift coffee stand and homemade cookies by volunteers. Guests endured the line-up for the toilet in the gardener's cabin, bypassing the portable toilet brought in for the day.

Veronica was ambivalent about visitors touring the garden. On the one hand, she wanted it to remain a peaceful and beautiful refuge for herself, family and friends. She did not want the "hoi polloi marching about" in the garden. On the other hand, she understood the need to open it to the public on a limited basis to produce the funds to maintain it. She talked about a gift shop at the "head of the driveway" that would sell tasteful souvenirs, art and books, reminiscent of the castle shop at Glin in Ireland. I always had the impression she would prefer that, as at Glin, use of the shop did not mean access to the garden.

Rudbeckia (coneflower).

Veronica's dear and loyal friend Mary Comber-Miles and her husband Victor, both artists, continued to be frequent visitors. Mary, a botanical illustrator of great repute, has a remarkable network of horticultural contacts throughout the world. She played a generous and tireless role in introducing the garden to her endless and serious contacts from the plant world, raising the profile and importance of the garden to international levels that would have been difficult to achieve otherwise.

Geoff Ball is a graduate of the Malaspina University-College horticulture program, hardworking, devoted and a skilled horticulturalist. He is, above all, a genuinely nice man. Geoff began to work at the garden as Horticulturalist in 1998, and over the years, has devoted many, many, many more hours than his contract demanded in this labour of love. In Veronica's time, Geoff would check in with the household staff in order to assess Veronica's mood and would plan his day accordingly. Veronica, he recalled, would often make small garden requests, perhaps to prune a particular hedge. He would drop everything and comply, in order, he said, to "keep the peace." Some of her requests were not, however, as simple to deal with. He recalled once being directed via the staff to "cut down all the shrubs on the front lawn," a request requiring far more diplomacy to decline.

During the first year we knew Veronica, she would drive me in a golf cart, rugs over our knees, the dog snuggled between us, to visit the garden. Later, as her health declined, Jim would drive the cart and I would wander along behind taking photographs. We spent many evenings on the veranda until dusk watching shadows grow across the lawn. The still white sun backlit cedars and Douglas-fir, making them glow. The colours of the sky changed from white to gold to red over the west. We often sat in silence, the gulls and loons crying in the distance; close to the house, perhaps a quail giving a distress call. At sunset, the birds would fall silent, leaving only the sound of waves against the shore. Sometimes, Veronica would sit on the veranda directing the pruning of trees so they were just right, framing a perfect view to the meadow.

Rich Johnston at Veronica's 89th birthday party in February, 1998.

Veronica had been born in the Edwardian era and lived almost until the end of the twentieth century. Many of her early and influential friends were Victorians. I spent many hours listening to her stories and harangues about the state of the modern world, especially the decline of the aristocracy and her idealized vision of the past. The British were, in her view, inherently superior, at the top of the evolutionary chain, the most advanced civilization in the world. The aristocracy was the "top of the top," and she was a member of this elite group. The duty of the British Empire was to elevate the colonies to British values of justice and prosperity. She was appalled by the rise of democracy. "The world is now ruled from the bottom!" she cried. She once told me that she would like to see a return to feudalism in which everyone knew his or her place. She, of course, would be on the top.

Her world view was often at odds with the reality of the modern world. Although she was interested in the world, she seemed to understand little of the lives of "ordinary people" in the late twentieth century. Some of this can be illustrated in her relationship with the University-College president. Rich Johnston had risen through the ranks at Malaspina. For twenty-four years, he typically signed correspondence to faculty and staff simply as "Rich," the name by which he is widely known. This absence of honorific, if noticed at all, seems to be generally viewed as a friendly gesture. Veronica, however, was appalled at this informality. "Imagine," she complained to me over and over again, "a man in his position behaving like that." It is, she said, "beyond jokes." She clearly viewed this as a serious character flaw in the president. It was so upsetting to her that she could not vocalize the word "Rich," and would

sputter and stumble in frustration. One day, I made the mistake of suggesting that perhaps he was attempting to be modern in approach. "Don't you defend him," she bristled. "You've met his mother and you know she didn't bring him up to behave that way!"

Veronica carried on the passionate debates that had been central to her development as an artist and gardener, especially those of the Celtic Revival. She retained an uncommon interest in the backgrounds of all she met, especially if they could be classified as Celt, Anglo-Saxon or Norman. She was passionate about intellectual debates almost a hundred years out of date, but was never able to articulate their context in a coherent manner. These interests and ideas, therefore, seemed entirely out of place in Canada in the late 1990s. Her views, especially her sense of inherent superiority and entitlement, were simply offensive to many.

To make matters worse, Veronica seemed to reinvent herself when it suited her. As one of her friends described it: "Veronica brought a lot of blarney with her from Ireland." Some fabrications were likely intentional, others more likely a result of old age, or even her lack of understanding of the modern world. Most often, Veronica's tendency to exaggeration or falsehood seemed to serve the purpose of enhancing her own image of herself and the world. Moreover, Veronica seemed well aware of this trait. Friends recall that she once silenced a dinner party by declaring that she was a "very good liar." When the queen visited, Veronica implied they had enjoyed dinners together and shared intimate conversations. She never admitted to me that she had actually had very little contact with the queen and was, in fact, not permitted on the property until the last hour of the visit. She clearly felt she should only associate with others of high status and would inflate the importance of those around her should she feel the need. She insisted on telling guests that I was closely related to former Governor General Vincent Massey. Much to his great embarrassment, Veronica introduced my husband as "descended from the high kings of Wales." While Cadwaladr was indeed the name of an ancient Welsh king, the link seemed to us more than a little tenuous. After all, the old king died in 664!

Veronica sometimes made unfounded allegations about those around her. She had the habit of abruptly breaking off relationships, often accusing the unfortunate of theft. Regrettably, this had the effect of alienating, or hurting, those who cared about her. In the end, she was left an isolated and vulnerable old woman. At times, she seemed to have some legitimate complaint about something. Her behaviour, however, had been so outrageous on so many occasions that she was not taken seriously, or her concerns were dismissed as mere ravings.

There are endless stories about Veronica. Many are true; many are false or exaggerated. Her arrogance made her an easy target for her actions to be interpreted in unflattering ways. Many of the stories involved her rude and impudent behaviour. Others concern her links to royalty: "The Queen, or the Queen Mother, was her friend." Some knew her as "Lady Veronica" or "Lady Milner." Although she never held a title, she would not discourage this form of address.

As I began to write this book, it became clear that Veronica's unusual personality reinforced the need to verify facts whenever possible. Sorting fact from fiction was never easy. As is often the case, there was usually some kernel of truth to what Veronica had to say. For example, she claimed her husband Ray Milner founded the Royal Bank of Canada. In fact, the bank was founded in Halifax in 1864 as the Merchants Bank and adopted the name Royal Bank of Canada in 1901 when Ray was twelve years old. Ray was, however, a member of the board of directors of the bank for twenty-five years.

Veronica talked about every imaginable subject. She had all the modern conveniences close at hand, including a TV and VCR. She was interested in the Internet and considered purchasing a computer in order to access it. To the end, she kept abreast of political affairs. During her final summer, U.S. President Bill Clinton's scandal with Monica Lewinsky was in the press. Veronica followed the troubles but could not understand what all the fuss was about. "Men in power have always done that," she said. And "Why was a twenty-year-old working in the White House anyway?"

In her last years, Veronica supported the Canadian Reform party. She had a strong and passionate belief in the freedom of the individual and abhorred state intrusion into private affairs. There were aspects of the party platform that clearly appealed to her. Yet Veronica's ideas were classically conservative and elitist rather than populist. She was concerned with preserving the inherited privilege and powers of the monarchy and landowners, limiting suffrage and preserving the old order. She had little in common with the Prairie populists and was becoming quickly disillusioned. Preston Manning (whom she had known for many years, as Ray was a friend of his father) needed to be "gotten rid of." She said this with such passion that I didn't like to ask how this might be accomplished.

Veronica maintained an unusual understanding of the world. She would jump from subject to subject. "The help are hopeless," the country is in ruins, the quails are in the garden; what is the nature of truth and beauty? What will be the results of space exploration on human evolution? She was an extremely intelligent woman who, like other women of her class and time, had very little formal education. Her world was based on observation and experience. She was interested in science, perhaps through the influence of her brother Amherst, a brilliant engineer and physicist. She had the advantage of knowing experts in several fields and was a talented artist. She had been a great beauty who had enjoyed

the admiration of many men, including those of some importance. Influential artists, garden experts and writers shaped her mind, in part, but she was unable to describe their contributions in any methodical fashion. For example, Veronica never explicitly described her garden to us as a "wild garden," nor mentioned her sources of inspiration, but many of her ideas clearly echoed those of William Robinson.

This out-of-the-ordinary juxtaposition of influences and inspirations made Veronica a fabulously creative and original thinker. A difficult, complex and unusual woman, she was both gifted and far-sighted. She took absolute delight in nature and anticipated trends toward the cultivation of native plants in the Canadian garden decades before they became popular. She absorbed the ideas of the great garden writer William Robinson and created a Canadian version of a "wild garden" in the rain forest, a teaching tool and living laboratory in a time when conservation was becoming increasingly important. This later contribution may become the crux of the garden's ongoing significance.

Always a woman of contradictions, Veronica retained her enduring interest in the unexplained, another carry-over from her association with figures in the Irish Revival of the early twentieth century. This interest in the paranormal took several forms: an interest in astrology, predestination, superstitions and, of course, fairies and the little people. Veronica believed that fairies lived underground in the garden near the glades. If you were still and quiet, you could feel their presence near the pools.

One evening in spring, I sat with Veronica while volunteers conducted tours in the garden. Veronica was excited about a lovely dream she had had. Beautiful maidens in white gowns, with long hair floating, danced across her dream. She told me she woke at 4 a.m. and read her bedside book, *In Tune With the Infinite,* her grandmother's personal compilation of devotions. And then it came to her. She would have a set of metal spiral stairs installed in a recessed area of the bedroom. "It would be wonderful," she declared. "With views over the Georgia Strait and the garden," she enthused.

Jim came in after the tours and she described the dream again. "Of course," she said matter-of-factly, "I might have to relocate my bedroom." Given her difficulties getting around without a walker, it was clear that the stairs were not for her use.

"Veronica, what would be the purpose of this?" my husband asked.

"Why to give the fairies free and easy access!" she declared as if it should be obvious.

Life in the house settled into a ritualistic pattern. Even her personal financial situation improved. She invested money on the stock market, "a miracle," she told me as the stocks rose. The garden grew vegetables for the house, fruits from the orchard, berries, rhubarb and French mint. Tea at four, served in the sitting room or on the veranda, was always served with the same small brass container containing artificial sweetener. A small, round dish with cookies for the dog, Willow. Dinner, too, was a ritual. Veronica, now needing help to get into her armchair at the head of the table, was still able to evoke another time and way of life. After dinner, if it were summer, we would sit on the veranda while the sun went down, the trees backlit by the evening sun.

We took Veronica on outings. Her reputation as a difficult, eccentric person, her larger-than-life aura and her presence, made her

the centre of attention wherever she went. Once we had lunch with her in a local restaurant. Veronica seemed unaware of the steady stream of people passing by our table, giving sideways glances. The chef, assorted waiters, the manager and customers all took peeks at our table.

She took great delight in the world around her. One Sunday evening at the end of March 1997, we had dinner with Veronica and friends. The sky had been heavy with rain and cloud for weeks. The fire and conversation were warm. Out on the lawn, the sky grew dark. Stars appeared for the first time in weeks. There across the sky appeared the Hale-Bopp comet, its trail across the navy sky brilliant white. Veronica was delighted.

October 31, 1997, we had dinner of pumpkin soup with curry, beets from the garden, carrots with basil, roasted potatoes and

free-range chicken with dressing. The candlelight reflected off the silver urn, the table with a Mexican frog and a crude but colourful bird. For dessert, puff pastry with chocolate and walnut sauce. Veronica was excited about a jack-o-lantern in the yard. After dinner, we watched until the candle burned out while we ate chocolates and drank coffee, Veronica staring intently at the flame as it flickered in the autumn wind.

She continued her difficult relationships with her staff. Many "helpers" and secretaries came and went with stunning rapidity. Yet, there was another side to her relationship with her staff. As one of her former Indian employees explained, there were both good and bad aspects of the job. He, in fact, held the family in such high regard that he named his eldest son "Milner." Veronica kept a framed photograph of her personal maid, Una Bourke, among photos of family and royalty in her sitting room. Late in life, she stunned long-time and long-exploited servant Nancy Ellis by telling her, "Nancy, I'm Veronica now to you, not Mrs. Milner." Nancy's reply to this incredible statement was, she said, "You've lost your marbles, Madame!"

Veronica was especially fond of Theresa, who had been her cook for many years, and demonstrated she could be kind and generous as well as rude and miserly. Theresa had had a stroke and was slowly recovering. Veronica visited her in the hospital and later at Trillium Lodge in Qualicum. She had her "helper" pick Theresa up and bring her to the house. Veronica sat in her wheelchair, and Theresa sat in hers, their knees almost touching as they drank tea from tipsy cups and ate cookies and tarts. Veronica praised Theresa: "She was a wonderful cook. We had beautiful times together." It was towards the end of summer and Theresa gave instructions for making plum wine. "We still have some of your lovely wine," Veronica told her.

One day Veronica told us that although she realized the garden no longer belonged to her, she was grateful that she was able to retain her home, to live her life as she pleased, without too much disruption. She had been worried about what the University-College takeover would mean. In the end, she came to trust that her beloved garden would be well cared for, and it was time to hand the garden on. Her garden was preserved. She seemed confident now about its future and left us well tutored about its meaning and care.

CHAPTER TEN

Endings

The Dormouse lay happy, his eyes were so tight
He could see no chrysanthemums yellow or white,
And all that he felt at the back of his head
Were delphiniums (blue) and geraniums (red).

—A.A. Milne

VERONICA'S HEALTH began to seriously decline. She had to rely on a walker and then a wheelchair. Her voice became very soft, apparently due to the thyroid problem. In February 1998, I found her propped in bed on pillows, tea placed at the foot of the bed for me. Veronica pointed out objects in the room. Photos of her mother and father, her children and grandchildren sat in a dusty jumble by her bed. She had a small flask of alcohol by the side of the bed. A hand-painted box full of cookies sat beside it. I seriously doubted that she would be able to attend her eighty-ninth birthday party planned for later that month. She gathered her strength for the event, however, and was at her most charming. Wearing a new teal dress, she toasted the garden and expressed her happiness with the way things were unfolding.

Throughout the spring and early summer, she took her tea on the veranda when she was able to. The camellias began to bloom,

tucked in the shade near the house, red, and variegated yellow; a pink bush bloomed by the veranda. Veronica was wrapped snugly under blankets. Birds worked at the feeder; a robin moved in the shrubs near the front of the house. The tea was hot and sweet. Veronica said proudly, "I'm an outdoor girl" as she gazed around her garden.

In August, she had surgery on her knee despite her advanced years. Veronica became depressed when she could no longer get out into the garden. "Better to die than live like this," she said. "What is the point of living if I can't go out into my garden?" She longed to re-

turn to Glin, but had been so difficult on her last visits that the family felt they could not tolerate her presence. Her son Desmond visited during the year and kept in touch by telephone and fax.

On November 5, 1998, some trees were still in splendid fall colour. There had been relatively little rain after a hot, dry summer. Leaves had fallen off other trees, first due to lack of rain, later the lessening sunshine. The garden receded, as red and yellow leaves floated on the pond; leaves piled up on the forest floor as the earth reclaimed them, taking them back bruised and blackening, the litter of the garden cycle.

As fog began to roll in, the sea became flat, lost in white light. The air smelled dank. Chestnuts (*Castanea sativa*) shattered prickly burrs to reveal shining nuts. The wisteria, now yellowed, sagged its way up a Douglas-fir standing on colourless grass. A few pieces of fruit that still had not fallen and a few late roses were clinging to their last days. Eucryphia, fuchsia and the myrtle near the door were blooming still. The rattan furniture from the veranda was stored against the coming winter rain.

It had been a dull day with soft rain off and on. From time to time, shafts of pale white sunlight slid across the orchard. By nightfall, the sky was brightening and the moonlit clouds formed black silhouettes of trees. Later, the clouds parted and the moon rose. Light spread across the sea. Stars appeared. An old lady died as the garden entered its winter rest.

Desmond came to her funeral and spread her ashes in the Qualicum garden. He took some of the ashes back to Glin, to spread in the Irish garden which she had done so much to create. Her pair of secateurs was buried in the family graveyard at St. Paul's church, where a single stone memorialises this remarkable woman. Her gardens in Ireland and Canada remain as her most lasting memorial.

Chapter Notes

The following sources were used in preparing this manuscript.

CHAPTER ONE

Sources used for plant identification include:

Brickell, Christopher (ed. in chief). *The Royal Horticultural Society Gardeners' Encyclopaedia of Plants and Flowers.* London: Dorling Kindersley, 1994.

Pojar, Jim and Andy McKinnon (eds.). *Plants of Coastal British Columbia including Washington, Oregon and Alaska.* Edmonton: Lone Pine Press, 1994.

Rushforth, Keith. *The Pocket Guide to Trees.* London: Mitchell Beazley, 1996.

Sunset Books and Sunset Magazine. *Sunset National Garden Book.* Menlo Park, Calif.: Sunset Books, 1997.

CHAPTER TWO

Several of Ray and Veronica's family members were of great help with this chapter.

Blake, Robert. *Disraeli.* New York: St. Martin's Press, 1966. 94.

Burke's Peerage. *Burke's Peerage and Baronetage.* London: Burke's Peerage, 1978. 558.

Canford School Archives. Untitled, undated printed material.

Cannadine, David. *Aspects of Aristocracy: Grandeur and Decline in Modern Britain.* New Haven and London: Yale University Press, 1994. 132, 133-137, 138, 139.

Cartland, Barbara. *We Danced All Night.* London: Hutchinson and Co., 1970. The romance novelist was a close contemporary of Veronica and both had similar backgrounds.

Cartwright, Julia. (ed.). *Journals of Lady Knightly of Fawsley 1856–1884.* (London 1916). Quoted in R.F. Foster. 16.

DeCandole, Nancy. Personal Interview with author. Errington, B.C. January 22, 1999.

Drabble, Margaret. (ed.). *Oxford Companion to English Literature,* 5th ed. Oxford: Oxford University Press, 1985. 53.

Fishman, Jack. *My Darling Clementine: The Story of Lady Churchill.* New York: David McKay, 1963.

FitzGerald, Desmond Windham Otho. Letters to Veronica Villiers (later FitzGerald), 1928–29. Unpublished.

———. Personal diaries, 1928–49.

Fleming, Kate. *The Churchills.* New York: The Viking Press, 1975. 22–23.

Foster, R.F. *Lord Randolph Churchill: A Political Life.* Oxford: Clarendon Press, 1981. 16.

Girouard, Mark. *Life in the English Country House: A Social and Architectural History.* New Haven and London: Yale University Press, 1978. 274, Plate 184.

Guest, Revel and Angela V. John. *Lady Charlotte: A Biography of the Nineteenth Century.* London: Weidenfeld and Nicholson, 1989. 26, 119, 120, 148. This biography is co-authored by Veronica's cousin, a BBC filmmaker.

Lacey, Robert. *Aristocrats.* Toronto: McClelland and Stewart, 1983. 16, 125.

Manchester, William. *The Last Lion: Winston Spencer-Churchill 1874–1932, Vision of Glory.* New York: Dell, 1983. 357, 401, 432, 643, 771.

Montague-Smith, Patrick (ed.). *Debrett's Peerage and Baronetage.* London: Debrett's Peerage, 1980.

Riley, Laura Date. "America's 10 Richest Women," *Ladies Home Journal,* September 1957. 60–61, 176, 178, 183.

Rose, Norman. *Churchill: An Unruly Life.* London: Simon and Schuster, 1994. 137.

Sampson, George. *The Concise Cambridge History of English Literature.* Cambridge: The University Press, 1965. 736.

Smith, Patricia. "Royal Retreat," *Monarchy Canada,* Winter 90-91. 12/13.

Taylor, Robert Lewis. *Winston Churchill: The Biography of a Great Man.* Montreal: Pocket Books of Canada, 1954. 48.

Villiers, Charles. Private conversation with author. Parksville, B.C. 1999.

Villiers, The Honourable Mrs. Elaine Augusta. Letters to Veronica FitzGerald, 1936–1945. Unpublished.

CHAPTER THREE

All diary entries are from the diaries of Desmond Windham Otho FitzGerald, 1925–48.

Adare Manor. A Potted History of Adare Manor. Co. Limerick: Ireland, http://www.adaremanor.ie/history.html. July 4, 2001.

Ardagh, John. *Ireland and the Irish: Portrait of a Changing Society.* London: Penguin, 1995. 176, 321.

Bence-Jones, Mark. *Life in an Irish Country House.* London: Constable, 1996. 16.

Burke, Sir Bernard. *Burke's Landed Gentry of Ireland.* London: Harrison and Sons, 1912.

FitzGerald, Olda. *Irish Gardens.* New York: Hearst, 1999. 135–143.

Glin Castle. *Glin Castle, Co. Limerick.* Undated.

Glin Castle. *Glin Castle Gardens: Brief History.* Limerick. Undated.

Foster, R.F. *Lord Randolph Churchill: A Political Life.* Oxford: Clarendon Press, 1981. 552.

Girouard, Mark. *Life in the English Country House: A Social and Architectural History.* New Haven and London: Yale University Press, 1978. 314.

Griffiths, Annabelle. Telephone interview. Langley, B.C. 1999.

Guinness, Desmond and William Ryan (eds.). *Irish Houses and Castles.* London: Thames and Hudson, 1971.

Knight of Glin. "The Awakening in Glin," *Irish Echo Supplement*, November 1997.

Knight of Glin. "My Mother" *Mothers* Dublin: Unicef, 1999.

Healy, Tom. Personal interview with author. Glin Castle. May 28, 2001.

Heron, Marianne. *The Hidden Gardens of Ireland*. Dublin: Gill and Macmillan, 2000. 36, 37.

Morton, HV. *In Search Of Ireland*. London: Methuen and Co., 1930. 62, 157.

O'Shaughnessy, John. "Some Recollections of Old Glin," *The Glencorbry Chronicle*. Glin Historical Society. Vol.1, No. 2, May 2001. 57.

CHAPTER FOUR

Bourke, Una. Letter to Veronica FitzGerald (later Milner), 1947.

Boylan, Henry. *A Dictionary of Irish Biography*. New York: Barnes and Noble, 1978.

Caldwell, Mark. *The Last Crusade: The War on Consumption 1862–1954*. New York: Atheneum, 1988. 246.

Ellis, Nancy. Personal interview with author. Ireland. May 27, 2001.

Father Browne's Homepage. *Frank Browne 1880–1960*. http://www.father browne.com. July 3, 2001.

Healy, Tom. Personal interview with author. Glin Castle. May 28, 2001.

Jacobs, Michael and Malcolm Warner. *The Phaidon Companion to Art and Artists in the British Isles*. Oxford: Phaidon Press, 1980. IR11.

Knight, Eve. Personal interview with author. Qualicum Beach. April 11, 1999.

Lamb, Keith and Patrick Bowe. *A History of Gardening in Ireland*. Dublin: National Botanic Gardens, 1995. 137, 149.

Leslie, Sir John Randolph (Shane). Letters to Veronica FitzGerald (later Milner), 1948–53, 1961.

Lovell, Mary S. *The Sound of Wings: The Life of Amelia Earhart*. New York: St. Martin's Press, 1989. 94.

Morton, HV. *In Search Of Ireland*. London: Methuen and Co. Ltd., 1930. 173.

National Gallery of Ireland. *Irish Women Artists from the Eighteenth Century to the Present Day*. Dublin: The National Gallery of Ireland, The Douglas Hyde Gallery, 1987. 35.

Nelson, Charles and Eileen McCracken. *The Brightest Jewel: A History of the National Botanic Garden, Glasnevin, Dublin*. Kilkenny, Ireland: Boethius Press, 1987. 213.

O'Driscoll, Robert. "Return to the Hearthstone: Ideals of the Celtic Literary Revival," in *Place, Personality and the Irish Writer*. Andrew Carpenter (ed.). Dublin: Harper and Row, 1977. 49.

Ryan, Frank, M.D. *The Forgotten Plague: How the Battle Against Tuberculosis was Won — And Lost*. Boston: Little, Brown and Co, 1992.

Walpole, E.H. . *Mount Usher 1868–1928: A Short History*. Dublin: n.p., 1929.

CHAPTER FIVE

Ray Milner's family was helpful in preparing this chapter.

Burke, Sir Bernard. *Burke's Landed Gentry of Ireland*. London: Harrison and Sons, 1912.

Cook, Alleyne. Private conversation with author. Qualicum Beach. 1999.

Cross, Archibald. Private correspondence, circa 1952.

Edmonton Journal. Ray was known as Mr. Alberta. He was often written about in Edmonton newspapers. "Retirement won't end love for city," April, 19, 1969. 3.

———. "Businessman H.R. Milner dies at Coast," May 26, 1975.

———. "Army Honours Milner," November 9, 1957. 23.

———. "Manning, Milner awarded medals," April 22, 1970.

Fraser, A.N. "Cottage for Mrs Bayley." Architectural Drawings. Qualicum Beach. Undated.

Golding, Jack. "The New Chancellor of Kings," publication unknown. circa 1957.

Greig, E.J. Letter to H.R. Milner. Royston, B.C., October 26, 1953.

———. Letter to Mr. Milner. Royston, B.C., September 27, 1953.

Greig, Jim and Jean. Personal interview with author. Nanoose Bay, BC. July 9, 1999.

Greig, Mary. "Mary Greig's story re Roys-ton Nursery." Unpublished manuscript, undated.

MacGregor, James G. *Edmonton: A History*. Edmonton: Hurtig Publishers, 1975. 178.

Macmillan, Margaret. *Women of the Raj*. London: Thames and Hudson, 1988. 11, 78. This book describes the private lives of British women in India during the British Empire and was useful in understanding how the architecture at the Milner house was influenced by life in colonial Sri Lanka.

Milner, H.R. Several carbon copies of letters from Ray Milner to Mary Greig, Ted Greig, Col. Nigel Bourke. Letters to E. J. Greig, Major Cross and caretaker Robert Strouts exist. They date from the late 1940s until 1953. Veronica's son Desmond very kindly asked the executors to give them to me for the purpose of writing this book. Several were used in the preparation of this chapter. The group contains copies of Ray's letter to W.H.M. Haldane, Q.C. December 1, 1952, and letter to contractor Don Beaton dated September 25, 1962. The Special Collections division of the University of Limerick contains letters from Ray to Desmond and Veronica FitzGerald, and letters to Veronica.

Milner, H.R. Letters to Robert Strouts, 1947–53.

———. Letter to W.H.M. Haldane, Q.C. December 1, 1952.

National Archives of Canada. Military Services Records. Canadian Expeditionary Forces. 1916–1975.

Palmer, Howard. *Alberta: A New History*. Edmonton: Hurtig Publishers, 1990. 78, 168.

St. John's Edmonton Report. "'Go west, H.R.,' said his aunt, and he did, and he prospered, and his life story is inseparable from the history of Edmonton." June 9, 1975. 6, 7.

Vircoe, Jeff. "Can Money's medals make their way home?" *The News Weekender*, Parksville, B.C., January 9, 1998. A3.

Wylie, Brad. *Qualicum Beach: A History of Vancouver Island's Best Kept Secrets*. Qualicum Beach: Brad Wylie, 1992. 45-46, 55.

CHAPTER SIX

Letters from H.R. Milner, as described in the notes to Chapter Five, were used in the preparation of this chapter.

Abbey, George. *Journal of Horticulture*, 1909, quoted in Clayton-Payne. 105.

Beaton, Don M. Letter to H.R. Milner, October 21, 1957.

Bothwell, Robert and William Kilbourn. *C.D. Howe: A Biography*. Toronto: McClelland and Stewart, 1979.

Bourke, Una. Letters to Veronica Milner, 1956–1963.

Clayton-Payne, Andrew. *Victorian Flower Gardens*. London: Weidenfeld and Nicolson, 1988. 76, 90.

Cook, Alleyne. "In Memoriam: Mary Greig," *Journal of the American Rhododendron Society*, Vol. 45, No. 1, Winter 1991.

Cowell, F.R. *The Garden as a Fine Art*. Boston: Houghton Mifflin, 1978.

Crockett, Edith. Letter to Mrs. H.R. Milner, December 4, 1969.

Eaton, Nicole and Hilary Weston. *In a Canadian Garden*. Markham, Ont: Viking Studio Books, 1989. 23, 24–25.

Ellis, Nancy. Personal interview with author. Ireland. May 27, 2001.

FitzGerald, Olda. "In Veronica's Garden." Unpublished notes, undated.

FitzGerald, Olda. Letter to Veronica Milner, 1974.

Gibson, William C. "Hippocrates' Home," reprinted from the *Journal of the American Medical Association*, Vol. 197, August 22, 1966. 628-631.

Greig, Jim and Jean. Personal interview with author. Nanoose Bay, B.C. July 9, 1999.

Knight, Eve. Personal interview with author. Qualicum Beach. April 11, 1999.

Meath, the Dowager Countess of. Personal interview with author. Killruddery House, Ireland. June 2, 2001.

Musk, George. *Canadian Pacific: The Story of the Famous Shipping Line*. Newton Abbot, London: David and Charles, 1981. 178.

Robinson, William. *The Wild Garden*. Portland, Ore: Sagapress/Timber Press, 1994. (Originally published 5th Ed. 1895). 14, 52, 137.

Ross, Stephanie. *What Gardens Mean*. Chicago: University of Chicago Press, 1998. xiii.

Vancouver Botanical Garden Association. "Minutes of the Board Meeting held in the Board Room of Canada Trust." Wednesday, June 13, 1973.

Villiers, The Honourable Mrs. Elaine Augusta. Letters to Veronica FitzGerald (later Milner), London circa 1953–1958.

Walker, Judith. Telephone interview with author. Comox, B.C. July 27, 2001.

Wall, Tom. Personal interviews with author. Glin Castle. May 26 and 27, 2001.

Yorath, D.K. "A Tribute to H.R. Milner," *The Courier*, Calgary: Public Relations Department, Canadian Western Natural Gas Co. and Northwestern Utilities, March 1962. 2.

CHAPTER SEVEN

Copps, Sheila. Letter to Veronica Milner, March 24, 1997.

Coren, Stanley. *Why We Love the Dogs We Do*. New York: Free Press, 1998. 2, 162.

Daily Telegraph. "Commander Clive Gwinner." March 14, 1998.

Eaton, Nicole and Hilary Weston. *In a Canadian Garden*. Markham, Ont: Viking Studio Books, 1989.

Farrow, Moira. "Queen-planted trees a must-see for mansion buyers," *The Vancouver Sun*, July 22, 1992. 3.

FitzGerald, Olda. "Carved From The Forest," *House and Garden*, March 1986. 140.

Gaude, G. Untitled Film. V.I. Productions, 1982.

Greig, Jim and Jean. Personal interview with author. Nanoose Bay, BC. July 9, 1999.

Hardin, Marguerite. "A Growing Passion," *Western Living*, May 1968. 65.

Hughes, Mary. Personal interviews with author. Port Alberni. 1998, 1999.

Kelly, Shauna. "Town protecting its trees," *The News*, July 18, 1995. 1.

Magnusson, Joan. Personal interview with author. Qualicum Beach. February 24, 1999.

Mount Arrowsmith Rhododendron Society Newsletter, Vol. 2 No. 5. Summer 1990.

Smythies, Charles O. Letter to Mrs. H.R. Milner, December 7, 1977.

University of Victoria. "Proposal for the Establishment of an International Centre for the Study of Global Change." Victoria, 1992.

Vander Zalm, Bill. Letter to Veronica Milner, March 17, 1986.

Van Versen, Lillian. Letters to Veronica Milner, circa 1947–52, 1957-63, 1964–67, 1968–84.

Villiers, Amherst. Letters to Veronica Milner, 1976–79, 1983-89.

Wall, Tom. Personal interviews with author. Glin Castle. May 26 and 27, 2001.

CHAPTER EIGHT

Campbell, Lady Colin. *Diana in Private*. New York: St. Martin's Press, 1992.

Charles, The Prince of Wales. Letter to Veronica Milner, May 5, 1986.

Cruikshank, John. "Contentious Commonwealth: Vancouver girds for politicians, protesters...and police," *The Globe and Mail*, October 10, 1987. 1

———. "Royal Couple retreat to private weekend after Victoria welcome, " *The Globe and Mail*, October 10, 1987. A5

Diana, Princess of Wales. Letter to Veronica Milner, May 5, 1986.

Farrow, Moira. "Hideaway awaits Royalty," *The Vancouver Sun*, October, 7, 1987. 1

Gibson, Jim. "This Town," *Victoria Times Colonist*, May 8, 1986.

———. "This Town," *Victoria Times Colonist*. October, 10, 1987. D1.

Harris, David. Telephone interview with author. Victoria. 2000.

Harris, Kenneth. *The Queen*. London: Weidenfeld and Nicolson, 1994. 242.

Holden, Anthony. *Charles*. Toronto: McClelland and Stewart Inc., 1989. 181.

Howard, Holly. "Secret Cruise," *The Province*, Vancouver, May 6, 1986. C5.

———. "Charles Takes a Cruise." *The Province*, Vancouver, May 6, 1986. 5.

Hughes, Mary. Personal interviews with author. Port Alberni. 1998, 1999.

Litwin, Grania. "Milner making way for Queen," *Victoria Times-Colonist*, October 9, 1987. B1.

―――. "Queen's visit short but sweet," *Victoria Times-Colonist*, October 10, 1987. 1

Magnusson, Joan. Personal interview with author. Qualicum Beach. February 24, 1999.

Morton, Andrew. *Diana: Her True Story*. New York: Simon and Schuster, 1997.55, 151.

Smith, Patricia. "Leo Teijgeman: Behind the scenes of a royal visit," *Monarchy Canada*, Spring/Summer, 1990. 18.

Sallot, Jeff. "Fiji and apartheid top summit talks," Toronto: *The Globe and Mail*, October 12, 1987. 1.

―――. "Amnesty cites 33 Commonwealth members," *The Globe and Mail*, October 12, 1987. 3.

The Nanaimo Times. " March 10 a Royal Nanaimo day." Tuesday, February 15, 1983. 1.

―――. "Our Royal Day." February 24, 1983.

Valpy, Michael and Jeff Sallot. "PM to promote South African sanctions," *The Globe and Mail*, October 12, 1987. 1.

CHAPTER NINE

Aylard, Richard. Letter to Veronica Milner, April 12, 1996.

Ellis, Nancy. Personal interview with author. Ireland. May 27, 2001.

Greig, Jim and Jean. Personal interview with author. Nanoose Bay, B.C. July 9, 1999.

Johnston, Richard W. Personal interview with author. Nanaimo, B.C. August 11, 2000.

―――.Letter to Veronica Milner, June 17, 1996.

―――.Letter to Veronica Milner, February 13, 1996.

Milner, Veronica. Letter to Prince Charles. Qualicum Beach, September 4, 1996.

Bibliography

Adare Manor. *A Potted History of Adare Manor.* Co. Limerick: Ireland. http://www. adaremanor.ie/history.html. July 4, 2001.

Albertan. Order of Canada given to Manning. Edmonton. April 23, 1970.

Ardagh, John. *Ireland and the Irish: Portrait of a Changing Society.* London: Penguin, 1995.

Arnold, Bruce. *The Art Atlas of Britain and Ireland.* London: Viking, 1991.

Arnold, Bruce. *Irish Art.* New York: Thames and Hudson, 1989.

Arrowsmith Star. "Royalty Drops in for Lunch." May 6, 1986. 1.

Augarde, Tony (ed.). *The Oxford Dictionary of Modern Quotations.* Oxford: Oxford University Press, 1991.

Austin, Alfred. *In Veronica's Garden.* London: Macmillan and Co, 1896.

———. *The Garden That I Love.* London: Macmillan and Co., 1894.

Aylard, Richard. Letter to Veronica Milner. London, April 12, 1996.

Beard, Madeleine. *Acres and Heirlooms: The Survival of Britain's Historical Estates.* New York: Routledge, 1989.

Beaton, Don M. Letter to H.R. Milner, October 21, 1957.

Bence-Jones, Mark. *Life in An Irish Country House.* London: Constable, 1996.

Blake, Robert. *Disraeli.* New York: St. Martin's Press, 1966.

Bothwell, Robert and William Kilbourn. *C.D. Howe: A Biography.* Toronto: McClelland and Stewart, 1979.

Bourke, Una. Letters to Veronica Fitz-Gerald (later Milner), 1947; 1953; 1956–63.

Boylan, Henry. *A Dictionary of Irish Biography.* New York: Barnes and Noble Books, 1978.

Bradford, Sarah. *Disraeli.* New York: Stein and Day, 1982.

Brickell, Christopher (ed. in chief). *The Royal Horticultural Society Gardeners' Encyclopaedia of Plants and Flowers (new ed.).* London: Dorling Kindersley, 1994.

Brown, Terence. *Ireland: A Social and Cultural History 1922 to the Present.* Ithaca N.Y.: Cornell University Press, 1985.

Burke, Sir Bernard. *Burke's Landed Gentry of Ireland.* London: Harrison and Sons, 1912.

Burke's Peerage. *Burke's Peerage and Baronetage.* London: Burke's Peerage, 1978.

Caldwell, Mark. *The Last Crusade: The War on Consumption 1862–1954.* New York: Atheneum, 1988.

Campbell, Lady Colin. *Diana in Private.* New York: St. Martin's Press, 1992.

Canford School Archives. Untitled, undated printed material.

Cannadine, David. *Aspects of Aristocracy: Grandeur and Decline in Modern Britain.* New Haven and London: Yale University Press, 1994.

Cartland, Barbara. *We Danced All Night.* London: Hutchinson and Co., 1970.

Cecil, Robert. *Life in Edwardian England.* London: BT Batsford, 1969.

Chase, Charles. Letter to William Beckingham, June 23, 1982.

Clayton-Payne, Andrew. *Victorian Flower Gardens.* London: Weidenfield and Nicolson, 1988.

Cook, Alleyne. "In Memoriam: Mary Greig," *Journal of the American Rhododendron Society.* Vol. 45, No. 1, Winter 1991.

Copps, Sheila. Letter to Veronica Milner, March 24, 1997.

Coren, Stanley. *Why We Love the Dogs We Do.* New York: The Free Press, 1998.

Cosier, Ralph. "Winnie's daughter Mary visits Qualicum Beach." *New Outlook for Seniors,* June 1984.

Cowell, F.R. *The Garden as a Fine Art.* Boston: Houghton Mifflin, 1978.

Courier. "Gathering Honours H.R. Milner." Calgary: Public Relations Department, Canadian Western Natural Gas Co. and Northwestern Utilities. Undated.

———. "Portrait of H.R. Milner now in board room." Calgary: Public Relations Department, Canadian Western Natural Gas Co. Ltd. and Northwestern Utilities. January 1968.

Crockett, Edith. Letter to Mrs. H.R. Milner. New York, December 4, 1969.

Cross, Archibald. Private correspondence. Circa 1952.

Cruikshank, John. "Contentious Commonwealth: Vancouver girds for politicians, protesters…and police," *The Globe and Mail,* October 10, 1987. 1.

———. "Royal Couple retreat to private weekend after Victoria welcome," *The Globe and Mail,* October 10, 1987. A5.

Cuthbertson, Yvonne. *Women Gardeners: A History.* Denver: Arden Press, 1998.

Daily Telegraph. "Commander Clive Gwinner." March 14, 1998.

Department of Botany, University of Alberta. Letter to Mrs. H.R. Milner, April 28, 1972.

Drabble, Margaret (ed.). *Oxford Companion to English Literature.* 5th ed. Oxford: Oxford University Press, 1985.

Drushka, Ken. *H.R.: A Biography of H.R. MacMillan.* Madeira Park, B.C.: Harbour Publishing, 1995.

Eaton, Nicole and Hilary Weston. *In a Canadian Garden.* Markham Ont: Viking Studio Books, 1989.

Edmonton Journal. "Businessman H.R. Milner dies at Coast." May 26, 1975.

———. "Manning, Milner awarded medals." April 22, 1970.

———. "Retirement won't end love for city." April 19, 1969. 3.

———. "Army Honours Milner." November 9, 1957. 23.

Elliot, David. "Qualicum began as elite haven," *The Times* (Nanaimo), February 22, 1983. 12A.

Ellis, Nancy. Letters to Veronica Milner. 1966–67.

Fallon, Brian. *Irish Art:1830–1990*. Belfast: Appletree Press, 1994.

Farrow, Moira. "Queen-planted trees a must-see for mansion buyers," *The Vancouver Sun*, July 22, 1992. 3.

———. "Hideaway awaits Royalty," *The Vancouver Sun*, October, 7, 1987. 1.

Father Browne's Homepage. *Frank Browne 1880-1960*. http://www.father browne.com. July 3, 2001.

Fishman, Jack. *My Darling Clementine: The Story of Lady Churchill*. New York: David McKay, 1963.

FitzGerald, Desmond John (see also Knight Of Glin). Letters to Veronica FitzGerald, (later Milner), 1945–1958, 1970–1985, 1990–1998.

FitzGerald, Desmond Windham Otho. Letters to Veronica Villiers (later Fitz-Gerald), 1928–29. 1946; 1947.

———. Personal Diaries, 1925-1949.

FitzGerald, Olda. "In Veronica's Garden." Unpublished notes, undated.

———. *Irish Gardens*. New York: Hearst, 1999.

———."Carved From The Forest," *House and Garden*, March 1986. 140.

———. Letters to Veronica Milner, Circa 1974–1976.

Flanagan, Mike. "The 50-year mystery of Amelia Earhart," *The Globe and Mail*. July 2, 1987. A7.

Fleming, Kate. *The Churchills*. New York: The Viking Press, 1975.

Foreman, Amanda. *Georgina: Duchess of Devonshire*. London: Harper Collins, 1998.

Foster, Lillian. "Fashion Was Winner Too," *The Toronto Telegram*, November 18, 1959. 31.

Foster, R.F. *Lord Randolph Churchill: A Political Life*. Oxford: Clarendon Press, 1981.

Fowler, Marian. *In A Gilded Cage: From Heiress to Duchess*. Toronto: Random House of Canada, 1993.

Fraser, A.N. "Cottage for Mrs Bayley." Architectural Drawings. Qualicum Beach, undated.

Free Press. "Noted rhodo grower dies." June 1990.

Frost, William (ed.). *Romantic and Victorian Poetry*. Englewood Cliffs, N.J.: Prentice-Hall, 1961.

Gaude, G. Untitled Film. V.I. Productions, 1982.

Gibson, Jim. "This Town," *Victoria Times-Colonist*, May 8, 1986.

Gibson, William C. "Hippocrates' Home," reprinted from the *Journal of the American Medical Association*. Vol. 197, 628–631, August 22, 1966.

Girouard, Mark. *Life in the English Country House: A Social and Architectural History*. New Haven and London: Yale University Press, 1978.

Glin Castle. *Glin Castle Gardens: Brief History*. Limerick. undated.

———. *Glin Castle, Co. Limerick*. undated.

Golding, Jack. "The New Chancellor of Kings," Publisher unknown, circa 1957.

Greene, B.M. (ed) *Who's Who in Canada*. Toronto: International Press, 1960-61.

Greig, E.J. Letter to H.R. Milner. Royston, B.C., October 26, 1953.

———. Letter to Mr. Milner. Royston, B.C., September 27, 1953.

Greig, Mary. Letter to H.R. Milner, 1953–64.

———. "Copy Plants sold". April 29, 1965.

———. Letters to Veronica Milner, 1957–1969.

———. "Mary Greig's story re Royston Nursery." Unpublished manuscript, undated.

Guest, Revel and Angela V. John. *Lady Charlotte: A Biography of the Nineteenth Century*. London: Weidenfeld and Nicholson, 1989.

Guinness, Desmond and William Ryan (eds.). *Irish Houses and Castles*. London: Thames and Hudson, 1971.

Hardin, Marguerite. "A Growing Passion," *Western Living*, May 1968. 65.

Harris, Jose. *Private Lives, Public Spirit: Britain 1870–1914*. London: Penguin Books, 1994.

Harris, Kenneth. *The Queen*. London: Weidenfeld and Nicolson, 1994.

Hastings, Selina. *Nancy Mitford: A Biography*. London: Hamish Hamilton, 1985.

Heron, Marianne. *The Hidden Gardens of Ireland*. Dublin: Gill and Macmillan, 2000.

Hibbert, Christopher. *Disraeli and His World*. New York: Charles Scribner's Sons, 1978.

Hilton, Timothy. *The Pre-Raphaelites*. London: Thames and Hilton, 1970.

Holden, Anthony. *Charles*. Toronto: Mc-Clelland and Stewart, 1989.

Horn, Pamela. *The Rise and Fall of the Victorian Servant*. Phoenix Mill, UK: Alan Sutton, 1990.

Howard, Holly. "Charles Takes a Cruise," *The Province* (Vancouver), May 6, 1986. 5.

———."Secret Cruise," *The Province* (Vancouver), May 6, 1986. C5.

Hughes, Mary. Letters to Veronica Milner, 1967–68; 1976; 1980.

Huxley, Anthony, (ed. in chief). *The New RHS Dictionary of Gardening*. Vols. 1–4. New York: Grove's Dictionaries, 1999.

Jacobs, Michael and Malcolm Warner. *The Phaidon Companion to Art and Artists in the British Isles*. Oxford: Phaidon Press, 1980.

Johnson, Bryan. "Tamils make mercy plea after battle," *The Globe and Mail*, October 12, 1987. 1.

Johnston, Richard W. Letter to Veronica Milner, June 17, 1996.

———. Letter to Prince Charles, March 11, 1996.

———. Letter to Veronica Milner, February 13, 1996.

Kellaway, Deborah. *The Virago Book of Women Gardeners*. London: Virago Press, 1995.

Kelly, Shauna. "Town protecting its trees," *The News* (Qualicum Beach), July 18, 1995. 1.

Kipling, Rudyard. "The Glory of the Garden," in Augarde. 125.

Knight of Glin (see also Desmond John FitzGerald). "My Mother" *Mothers*. Dublin: Unicef, 1999.

———. "The Awakening in Glin," *Irish Echo Supplement*, November 1997.

Lacey, Robert. *Aristocrats.* Toronto: McClelland and Stewart, 1983.

Lamb, Keith and Patrick Bowe. *A History of Gardening in Ireland.* Dublin: National Botanic Gardens, 1995.

Leslie, Anita. *The Marlborough House Set.* New York: Doubleday, 1973.

Leslie, Sir John Randolph (Shane). Letters to Veronica Milner, 1948–53, 1961.

Litwin, Grania. "Queen's visit short but sweet," *Victoria Times-Colonist*, October 10, 1987. 1.

———. "Milner making way for Queen," *Victoria Times-Colonist*, October 9, 1987. B1.

Lovell, Mary S. *The Sound of Wings: The Life of Amelia Earhart.* New York: St. Martin's Press, 1989.

Lund, C.E. *Miscellaneous Verse, Readings, Recitations, Songs and Hymns.* Toronto: T.H. Best Co., 1926. 8.

MacDonald, W.L. and F.C. Walker. *A Selection of English Poetry.* Toronto: J. M. Dent and Sons, 1964.

MacGregor, James G. *Edmonton: A History.* Edmonton: Hurtig Publishers, 1975.

Macmillan, Margaret. *Women of the Raj.* London: Thames and Hudson, 1988.

Malone, Ted (ed.). *The Pocket Book of Verse.* Montreal: Pocket Books of Canada, 1945.

Manchester, William. *The Last Lion: Winston Spencer-Churchill 1874–1932: Vision of Glory.* New York: Dell, 1983.

Mason, Haldane. *Through Irish Eyes: A Visual Companion to Angela McCourt's Ireland.* New York: Smithmark, 1998.

McCarter, Alex. (ed.). *Rhododendrons On A Western Shore.* Victoria: The Victoria Rhododendron Society, April 1989.

McConkey, Kenneth. *A Free Spirit: Irish Art 1860–1960.* London: Antique Collectors' Club in association with Pyms Gallery, 1990.

Milne, A.A. "The Doctor and the Dormouse." *The World of Christopher Robin.* Toronto: McClelland and Stewart, 1983. 81.

Milner, H.R. Letter to Don Beaton, September 25, 1962.

———. Letter to E.L. Halliday, March 14, 1961.

———. Letters to E. J. Grieg, Sept. 17; November 4, 1953.

———. Letter to Mary Greig, March 30, 1953.

———. Letter to Major Cross, September 8; December 23, 1952.

———. Letter to W.H.M. Haldane, Q.C., December 1, 1952.

———. Letters to Veronica FitzGerald, 1948, 1953–54.

———. Letters to Robert Strouts, 1947–53.

———. Letter to Col. Nigel Bourke, Undated.

Milner, Veronica. Letter to Prince Charles, Sept. 4, 1996.

———. Letter to Sheila Copps, August 26, 1996.

———. Letter to Prince Charles, March 8, 1996.

———. Notes for Acceptance of Honorary Degree for Mary Greig. June 1991.

———. Letter to Prince Charles. Undated, circa 1989.

———. Letters and notes re National Trust for Ireland, 1953.

———. Various Personal correspondence.

Montague-Smith, Patrick (ed.). *Debrett's Peerage and Baronetage.* London: Debrett's Peerage, 1980.

Morrogh, Michael MacCarthy. *The Irish Century: A Photographic History of the Last Hundred Years.* Niwot, Col.: Robert's Rinehart Publishers, 1998.

Morton, Andrew. *Diana: Her True Story.* New York: Simon and Schuster, 1997.

Morton, H.V. *In Search Of Ireland.* London: Methuen and Co., 1930.

Mount Arrowsmith Rhododendron Society Newsletter. Vol. 2, No. 5. Parksville, B.C.: Summer 1990.

Musk, George. *Canadian Pacific: The Story of the Famous Shipping Line.* Newton Abbot, London: David and Charles, 1981.

National Archives of Canada. *Military Services Records. Canadian Expeditionary Forces, 1916–1975.*

National Gallery of Ireland. *Irish Women*

Artists From the Eighteenth Century to the Present Day.* Dublin: The National Gallery of Ireland, The Douglas Hyde Gallery, 1987.

Nelson, Charles and Eileen McCracken. *The Brightest Jewel: A History of the National Botanic Garden, Glasnevin, Dublin.* Kilkenny, Ireland: Boethius Press, 1987.

Nilsson, Sten. *European Architecture in India 1750–1850.* New York: Taplinger Publishing Company, 1968.

Nowlan, Kevin and T. Desmond Williams. *Ireland In the War Years and After 1939–51.* Notre Dame, Ind.: University of Notre Dame Press, 1969.

O'Driscoll, Robert. "Return to the Hearthstone: Ideals of the Celtic Literary Revival." in *Place, Personality and the Irish Writer.* Andrew Carpenter (ed.). Dublin: Harper and Row, 1977.

O'Shaughnessy, John. "Some Recollections of Old Glin." in *The Glencorbry Chronicle.* Glin Historical Society. Vol. 1, No. 2, May 2001.

Osler, Mirabel. *In the Eye of the Garden.* London: JM Dent, 1993.

———. *A Gentle Plea for Chaos: The Enchantment of Gardening.* New York: Simon and Schuster, 1989.

Ottawa Citizen. "Order of Canada honors to 28." April 22, 1970. 2.

Palmer, Howard. *Alberta: A New History.* Edmonton: Hurtig, 1990.

Peterson, Paul. Letter to C.O. Smythies, June 11, 1982.

Phillips, Alan. "Who Will Win The Great Gas Pipeline Stakes?" *Macleans Magazine*, October 1, 1953. 18.

Plumb, J.H. *Royal Heritage: The Story of Britain's Royal Builders and Collectors.* London: British Broadcasting Corporation, 1977.

Pojar, Jim and Andy McKinnon (eds.). *Plants of Coastal British Columbia including Washington, Oregon and Alaska.* Edmonton: Lone Pine Press, 1994.

Prince of Wales, The. Letter to Veronica Milner, May 5, 1986.

Provincial Archives, Province of British Columbia. *Bright Sunshine and a Brand New Country.* Victoria: Queen's Printer, 1979.

Putman, George Palmer. *Soaring Wings: A Biography of Amelia Earhart*. New York: Harcourt, Brace and Co., 1939.

Riley, Laura Date. "America's 10 Richest Women," *Ladies Home Journal*, September 1957. 60–61, 176, 178, 183.

Robbins, Maria Polushkin. *A Gardener's Bouquet of Quotations*. New York: Dutton, 1993.

Robinson, William. *The Wild Garden*. Portland, Ore: Sagapress/Timber Press, 1994. (Originally published as 5th ed. 1895.)

Rose, Norman. *Churchill: An Unruly Life*. New York: Simon and Schuster, 1994.

Ross, Stephanie. *What Gardens Mean*. Chicago: University of Chicago Press, 1998.

Ruissen, J. Appraisals Ltd. *Report to W. Beckingham and Co*. "Appraisal of Two Residential Lots." Port Alberni. 1982.

Rushforth, Keith. *The Pocket Guide to Trees*. London: Mitchell Beazley, 1996.

Ryan, Frank, M.D. *The Forgotten Plague: How the Battle Against Tuberculosis was Won — And Lost*. Boston: Little, Brown and Co., 1992.

Sallot, Jeff. "Fiji and apartheid top summit talks," Toronto: *The Globe and Mail*, October 12, 1987. 1.

———. "Amnesty cites 33 Commonwealth members," Toronto: *The Globe and Mail*, October 12, 1987. 3.

Sampson, George. *The Concise Cambridge History of English Literature*. Cambridge: The University Press, 1965.

Saskatoon Star-Phoenix. "Big Quick Freeze Plant Opened." Saskatoon: October 21, 1955.

St. John's Edmonton Report. "'Go west, H.R.', said his aunt, and he did, and he prospered, and his life story is inseparable from the history of Edmonton." June 9, 1975. 6.

Smith, Patricia. "Royal Retreat," *Monarchy Canada*, Winter 90–91. 12–13.

———. "Leo Teijgeman: Behind the scenes of a royal visit," *Monarchy Canada*, Spring/Summer 1990.

Smythies, Charles O. Letter to Mrs. H.R. Milner, December 7, 1977.

Steer, Mrs. George. Letter to Veronica Milner, 1958.

Strong, David. "Citation Read on the occasion of the granting of the degree of Honorary Doctor of Science to Mary Greig by the Senate of the University of Victoria." Victoria B.C., University of Victoria. June 1, 1991.

Strouts, Nita. Letter to Mr. Milner, November 15, 1953.

Strouts, Robert. Letters to H.R. Milner, 1947–53.

———. Letter to Miss Chisholm, April 6, 1947.

Sunset Books and Sunset Magazine. *Sunset National Garden Book*. Menlo Park, Calif.: Sunset Books, 1997.

Tan, Emma (ed.). *Ireland*. New York: Prentice Hall, 1994.

Taylor, Robert Lewis. *Winston Churchill: The Biography of a Great Man*. Montreal: Pocket Books of Canada, 1954.

Teasdale, Sara. "Advice to a Girl." in Malone. 243.

Tennyson, Alfred Lord. "Crossing the Bar." In MacDonald and Walker. 104.

———. "'The Gardener's Daughter." in Robbins. 105.

The Times (Nanaimo). "March 10 a Royal Nanaimo day." Tuesday, February 15, 1983. 1.

———. "Our Royal Day." February 24, 1983.

Thompson, Paul. *The Edwardians: The Remaking of British Society*. Chicago: Academy Publishers, 1985.

Thwaites, E.D. Letter to Provincial Assessor, January 12, 1959.

Trine, Ralph Waldo. *In Tune With the Infinite: Fullness of Reace, Power and Plenty*. London: Thorsons, 1995. (First published 1899). 103.

Twigg, Alan. *Vander Zalm: From Immigrant to Premier*. Madeira Park, B.C: Harbour Publishing, 1986.

University of King's College. "King's Chancellor-Elect Distinguished Industrialist." Halifax: University of King's College, November 1957.

University of Victoria. "Proposal for the Establishment of an International Centre for the Study of Global Change." Victoria, 1992.

Valpy, Michael and Jeff Sallot. "PM to promote South African sanctions," *The Globe and Mail*, October 12, 1987. 1.

Vancouver Botanical Garden Association. "Minutes of the Board Meeting held in the Board Room of Canada Trust." Wednesday, June 13, 1973.

Vander Zalm, Bill. Letter to Veronica Milner, March 17, 1986.

Villiers, Amherst. Letters to Veronica Milner, 1954–58, 1976–79, 1983–89.

Villiers, The Honourable Mrs. Elaine Augusta. Letters to Veronica FitzGerald (later Milner), 1936–1945, 1953–1958.

Vircoe, Jeff. "Can Money's medals make their way home?" *The News Weekender* (Parksville, B.C.), January 9, 1998. A3.

Von Versen, Lillian. Letters to Veronica Milner, circa 1947–52, 1957–63, 1964–67, 1968–84.

Walpole, E.H. *Mount Usher 1868–1928: A Short History*. Dublin: np, 1929.

Waterson, Merlin (ed.). *The Country House Remembered: Recollections of Life Between the Wars*. London: Routledge and Kegan Paul, 1985.

Webb, R.K. *Modern England: From the 18th Century to the Present*. New York: Dodd, Mead and Co., 1979.

Welsh, Robert (ed.). *Irish Writers and Religion*. Gerrard's Cross: Colin Smythe, 1992.

Wylie, Brad. *Qualicum Beach: A History of Vancouver Island's Best Kept Secrets*. Qualicum Beach: Brad Wylie, 1992.

Wylie, John. "28 Invested Into Order of Canada," *The Ottawa Journal*, April 22, 1970. 25.

Yeats, W.B. "The Stolen Child." *Fairy Tales of Ireland*. Dublin: Roberts Wholesale Books, 2000.

———. "Aedh Wishes for the Cloths of Heaven." In Augarde. 235.

Yorath, D.K. "A Tribute to H.R. Milner," *The Courier*, Calgary: Public Relations Department, Canadian Western Natural Gas Co. Ltd. and Northwestern Utilities, March, 1962.

Photo Credits

With the following exceptions, all photographs in this book are by the author, Margaret Cadwaladr.

Collection of Veronica Milner: Pages 14, 19, 32, 37,46, 73, 77, 85, 90, 94, 102, 103, 105, 108, 111 (top left), 114, 122, 128 (lower right), 129, 130, 139,156, 157, 167, 180 (left), 181, back cover.

Courtesy of Desmond FitzGerald: Pages 28, 29 (top), 45, 47, 50, 51, 52, 53, 95, 106.

Courtesy of Judith Walker: Page 135.

Courtesy of Nancy deCandole: Page 21.

Courtesy of Elizabeth Mewburn: Page 86.

Courtesy of Jim and Jean Grieg: Page 96.

Photo by Margaret Masse Page: xxi.

Photos by John Lund, Malaspina University-College: Pages: 174,175.

Photos by Jim Cadwaladr: Page 180 (right), cover photo of author.

© Global Geometrics, Qualicum Beach, B.C. used with permission. Page xiii.

© Adare Manor Hotel and Golf Resort, used with permission. Page 38.

© Vancouver Sun, used with permission Page 137.

Index

Page references in italics indicate photographs or illustrations.